Secrets Men Keep

Secrets
MEN KEEP

Stories by
Ron Rindo

Minnesota Voices Project Number 71

New Rivers Press 1995

New Rivers Press is a non-profit literary press dedicated to publishing the very best emerging writers in our region, nation, and world.

The publication of *Secrets Men Keep* has been made possible by generous grants from the Dayton Hudson Foundation on behalf of Dayton's and Target Stores, the Jerome Foundation, the Metropolitan Regional Arts Council (from an appropriation by the Minnesota Legislature), the North Dakota Council on the Arts, the South Dakota Arts Council, and the James R. Thorpe Foundation.

Additional support has been provided by the Bush Foundation, the General Mills Foundation, Liberty State Bank, the McKnight Foundation, the Minnesota State Arts Board (through an appropriation by the Minnesota Legislature), the Star Tribune/Cowles Media Company, the Tennant Company Foundation, and the contributing members of New Rivers Press. New Rivers Press is a member agency of United Arts.

New Rivers Press books are distributed by The Talman Company, 131 Spring Street, Suite 201 E-N, New York, NY 10012 (1-800-537-8894).

Secrets Men Keep has been manufactured in the United States of America for New Rivers Press, 420 N. 5th Street/Suite 910, Minneapolis, MN 55401. First Edition.

Acknowledgments

"Eclipse" appeared in *Clockwatch Review;* "Cyclone Eddie King" appeared in *The Boundaries of Twilight: Czecho-Slovak Writing from the New World* (New Rivers Press, 1991); "The Summer I Learned Baseball" appeared in *Wisconsin Academy Review;* "Aliens" appeared in *Story.* We wish to thank the editors of these publications for permission to reprint these stories in *Secrets Men Keep.*

FOR ELLEN
WHO LIVES WITH MY SECRETS,
AND FOR CLAIRE AND TY,
WHO KEEP NONE.

Contents

Eclipse

THAT SPRING, their best friends, Olivia and John, had invited Michael and Angela to see a performance artist at the avant-garde theatre downtown. Theatre X, it was called, the large X painted black against a white background, just out of focus, like a chromosome under a powerful microscope. A young man with thinning hair and a skeletal face stood on stage, facing the audience, wearing a long overcoat made from morsels of chipped beef glued to mesh netting with maple syrup. (This coat weighed seventeen pounds and had to be kept in a refrigerator prior to the performance.) On four sides of him were covered, black wooden boxes. These boxes were filled with rats. Nine hundred and twelve rats in all, Michael and Angela later learned. They could hear the greasy feet and yellowed teeth scraping against the wood. Behind the man, on risers, was a choir of male and female acting students, all nude, holding candles. When the lights were snapped off, the wooden boxes fell open, and rats, white, black, and brown, streamed across the stage toward the artist, who stared straight ahead, arms raised as if in crucifixion. The choir chanted, over and over, "Naked and alone, we came into exile," in a rising crescendo, as the rats flowed up the overcoat like flames, leaping and climbing and devouring. Soon the man was wearing a squirming coat of rats. The weight caused him to drop his arms and stagger toward the audience. Michael and Angela were in the second row, and they could hear

1

the hum of the feeding, the frenzied cries of the rats' angry hunger. Michael could smell the beef and the maple syrup. Within minutes, whole pieces of the coat fell away, and it wasn't long until the man stood naked and the rats streamed up the red velvet stage curtains, a living tapestry of swarming vermin.

Then, in an impromptu continuation of the performance—which is what made it such a memorable piece of art, Olivia insisted later, over cappuccino—the rats began to drop off the stage, a few at a time, to scurry into the audience. In the darkness, an uneasy chatter preceded general panic, as the still-hungry animals nipped shoes and ankles, and got their incisors stuck in black fishnet hose, in spandex and faded denim, in leather flight jackets. In the hurried retreat to the lobby, with Michael pushing Angela ahead of him, and members of the audience screaming "Lights! Lights!," a white rat with pink eyes bit through Michael's back pocket and into his wallet, puncturing a twenty-dollar bill.

Later, they read that these rats had been denied food for nine days. A representative of the SPCA at the performance had written an editorial accusing the artist of starving the animals for artistic purposes. The artist, it turned out, had been bitten many times. So had several members of the audience. They were forced to undergo rabies shots because no one knew if all of the animals had been disease-free. Maintenance personnel, student volunteers, and several members of the audience spent five hours recapturing the rats in long-handled nets, and ended up with eight hundred and two. One hundred and ten could not be found.

That night, as they drove back to the apartment they shared overlooking Lake Michigan, Angela told Michael that she was pregnant.

His mouth suddenly dry, his palms sticky, Michael panicked. Later, he could not remember which of his reactions had merely flashed in his mind, and which had been spoken: Are you sure. How long have you known. You had to know it would upset me or you wouldn't have waited this long to tell me. What are we going to do. How could this happen.

What are we going to do?

They fell asleep back to back in the waterbed, curled into fetal commas, only the sharp slabs of their scapulas—like scalpels, Michael thought—touching. They had been together for eight months, sleeping together for seven. And now this.

~

IT—they would refer to the pregnancy as IT for some time— happened the night of the Chinese acrobats. They determined this while lying on their backs, shoulder to shoulder, in the morning, retracing the month's history. Angela had already figured it out. Michael could tell by the way she led him to it, like dropping a trail of bread crumbs.

The Chinese Acrobats of Peking. Eight men and six women in red uniforms who controlled each muscle cell in their bodies. Michael and Angela watched them in awe. The crowd applauded loudest for the most outlandish tricks: all fourteen acrobats stacked in a human pyramid on a moving bicycle; one man balanced on another, one standing on the stage, the other, in a mirror image, straight above him, their bodies connected only by the tips of the knives they held in their teeth.

Later, Michael and Angela talked over their favorites. For Angela, it was the woman who balanced on chairs. This began with a simple handstand on a single ladderback chair, then progressed as more and more chairs were passed up to her. Each time, she added a chair—on its side, upside down, on an angle—to the stack, and climbed higher. As she added the tenth chair, and performed a handstand on top of it, her legs disappeared above the ruffle of the stage curtain.

Michael's favorite act was earthbound. A thin, attractive woman— probably a girl of sixteen or seventeen—began with a single, silver tray of twelve long-stemmed wine glasses, each glass half filled with red wine. Slowly, accompanied by soft stringed music, she lay on her stomach, holding the tray over her shoulder, balanced on one hand. Another tray, with twelve more glasses, was added to her other hand, then one on the bottom of each foot, then one on her head. She held five trays in all, sixty wine glasses. Her back was arched until only her stomach rested on the floor. Then so slowly she seemed not to be moving at all, she raised herself to her knees, then shifted positions until she was on her back, her chin tucked into her chest, her legs and arms stiff, all five silver trays still perfectly balanced.

When the act was completed, the wine was passed to members of the audience sitting in the front rows.

When Michael and Angela made love that night, he imagined the

Chinese girl in her red body stocking. He and Angela had barely made it through the door when their mouths came together hard. Michael forced Angela against the wall, pinning her arms behind her back as she struggled out of her coat. He could feel the bones of her hips against the top of his thighs, the warm skin of her back, the soft knots of her spine. Soon their clothes were scattered on the apartment floor, his body was pressed into hers, and they rocked together and competed for leverage.

They rolled once and Angela was on top of him, sliding against him, her forehead touching his. She licked his lips and bit him gently on the chin. Her tongue tasted of cappuccino, and Michael smelled the pleasant apricot fragrance of her hair spray. He sat up and lifted her with him, her legs wrapped around his back, raised himself to his knees, and lunged awkwardly for the couch, toppling it over. They both laughed and rolled to the floor. He was still inside of her. Angela bit him on the lip teasingly, and he rolled back on top of her.

Soon, Angela was yelling and laughing as she thrashed beneath him, one of her knees driving into his back. Her body folded around his like an envelope. His own body convulsed in pleasurable spasms, and he leaned into her, pinning one of her thighs against his ribs with one arm as he thrust against her. The muscles in his back burned. When he rolled off of Angela, she smiled and rested her head on his arm. They fell asleep listening to the traffic on the street below.

Michael hadn't asked, but he assumed Angela was about to have her period or had been wearing something—a sponge, probably. The Pill gave Angela blood clots in her legs, so they shared contraceptive responsibility. He knew it was one of the things she liked about him. He kept condoms in the nightstand. He'd even sent away for some exotic rubbers from Brazil, zebra-striped condoms that glowed in the dark. These made him look like a giant, reticulated caterpillar. Angela kept her diaphragm in the bathroom. It had to be custom-fit at the doctor's office. Angela sometimes teased Michael, saying that one cock is the same as the next, one size fits all, but a woman requires custom-designed latex, that the entrance to her womb is as unique as a fingerprint.

But there had been nothing between them that night.

∼

The earliest she could get an appointment, Angela went to her doctor. A urine test confirmed the pregnancy.

"When she said 'Congratulations, you're pregnant!' I felt nauseous, but I smiled," Angela said. "I wasn't pretending either. It just came out on its own. Then I threw up in one of those little plastic dishes shaped like a kidney." She wiped the corners of her mouth with a tissue.

"So what are you saying?" Michael asked. They had left the waiting room and were walking to the car.

"I'm not saying anything," Angela said. "I couldn't help myself. It doesn't *mean* anything." She looked up into his face, and he forced a smile back at her. He could tell it was not the smile Angela wanted to see, and she looked away.

They did not speak as Michael guided the car down through the circular, concrete tunnels of the parking structure. When he had safely merged into the rush-hour traffic on Michigan Street, Michael looked at Angela. "So when are we going to take care of it?"

"I don't want it either, Michael, okay?" Angela snapped. "But I don't want to be rushed. Just don't rush me." She turned on the radio and put her seat belt on.

For a moment, Michael felt vaguely like the man in a Hemingway story he had read in his college literature class. It came out of the air, the memory of it, the classroom, the desk in the back where he always sat, the professor, a woman who clicked her fingernails on the desk when no one had read the assignment. The title of this story was something about white elephants, although there weren't any elephants in it. A man was talking to his girlfriend in a restaurant. He was trying to talk her into having an abortion, but he was talking around it, hinting, telling her there was nothing to it. He never used the word "abortion," but the woman understood everything. She was upset, but the man didn't seem to notice.

Michael and Angela had never used that word either. They danced around it, a euphemistic tango, a tangle of uncommitted speculation. Michael did not want to have a baby. But he could not say it.

At lunch the following day he drove to the downtown library. The reference librarian directed him to a collection of Hemingway's stories. The story he remembered was called "Hills Like White Elephants." He checked the book out and read the story in his car. As he read, he found himself getting more and more nervous. He had to think about breathing, as if his diaphragm were no longer an involuntary muscle.

When he finished the story, he returned the book to the night depository and drove back to work.

~

The Buddhist in a jar.

At the end of May, Michael and Angela went with Olivia and John to watch a man survive thirty minutes under water without scuba gear. This event was sponsored by the Alternative Lifestyles group John belonged to at the university. AL had previously offered seminars in vegetarianism (John's interest), organic gardening, and holistic healing. Held at the university aquatic center, a cavernous, brown brick auditorium thick with the smell of chlorine, this seminar was entitled *Eastern Discipline for Body and Soul*.

The first half of the program was a lecture, "Zen and You," delivered by an aging professor wearing earth shoes and a long, gray ponytail. He urged listeners to find room for Eastern Philosophy in their busy Western lives, pointing out that in addition to the peace of mind this had offered him, his blood cholesterol level had dropped from two hundred eighty-three to one hundred seventy-one. Michael watched Angela as he listened to the lecture. She sat with one hand across her stomach, occasionally moving the tips of her fingers along the surface of her blouse.

The program's second half was a tour de force. A young man with dark skin who claimed to be from Tibet was introduced to the audience. When he removed his robe, he was wearing a pair of red swimming trunks. The lights were turned off, leaving the room illuminated only by the pool's underwater lights, which gave the air an eerie, greenish glow. By the side of the pool stood a plexiglass box, approximately three feet by three feet, with a hinged, watertight cover. Accompanied by sitar music which echoed from the tinny sound system, the young man sat down on the gray tile and meditated, breathing deeply and slowly, his eyes closed. When he was prepared, approximately ten minutes later, he carefully folded his body into the plexiglass box. His flesh flattened against it from the inside. When he tucked his head in front of his knees, two men in swimming trunks closed the box, walked it into the pool, and placed it on the bottom, five feet down. Beside the pool, a large white clock with a sweeping second hand was started, facing the audience.

Michael looked at Angela. She was reclined against the bleachers behind her, hands folded across her stomach, fingers interlocked.

Under the water, folded and shining in the light, the young man waited.

Twenty minutes into the program, the sitar music stopped. A small light was switched on at the lecturn, and the professor who had given the earlier lecture explained what everyone was witnessing. The young man in the pool could instruct the rhythms of his brain and his body to slow down, to demand less oxygen. He became like a pupa inside a chrysalis. In the thirty minutes he would be under water, his heart would beat six times. He would breathe just twice. Every large muscle group in his body would be so relaxed it would have the density of a thick liquid, such as honey. When he emerged from this state, he would have acquired the metabolic benefits of eight hours of sleep.

The sitar music came on again.

The Buddhist in the jar was retrieved from the pool and set before the audience. He emerged slowly, each limb unfolding. Michael kept expecting to see wings, though he knew that was ridiculous. The young man did not have wings. But he smiled broadly and bowed, and Michael clapped until his hands tingled.

That night in the apartment, as he reached for a towel beneath the bathroom sink, Michael found a thick, paperback book entitled, *What To Expect When You're Expecting*.

"What the hell is this?" He dropped it on the bed. Angela picked it up and tucked it under her arm.

"A book I'm reading," Angela said. "I just want to know what I'm dealing with here, that's all."

"And what are you dealing with?"

"Something that looks like a chicken embryo right now. There's a little heart beating, too. You want to see the picture?"

"Oh, this is just great," Michael said. "This is fucking great, Angela." He hurried back into the bathroom and closed the door. He sat down on the toilet cover, crossed his arms, and jiggled a leg nervously. He stood and ran cold water on his hands, then rubbed them against his face. He brushed his teeth.

When he came out, Angela was sitting cross-legged in bed, waiting.

"Michael, we talk about everything else, why can't we talk about this?"

"How do you talk about this? You tell me. What do we say?"

"We do what we always do."

"No," Michael said. "That's not what's happening here. I know this sounds wrong but usually the guy has a little bit more control. I mean I know that's not perfect, but that's what I'm used to. I'm nowhere here, Angela. I don't think you know what that feels like."

"Look, if you don't want to have it we won't have it. I won't. I wouldn't do that."

Michael calmed, hearing this. But he tried not to seem relieved. He knew relief would make Angela angry.

"Well, what do you want?"

"See, that's the thing. I don't know. We don't need this right now, I know that. If you want me to take care of this, then I will. Then maybe that's the best thing."

"What would that do to us?" Michael asked.

"What do you mean?"

"Who would we be, then?"

"We'd be different, Michael," Angela said. "We'll be different either way."

Michael didn't say anything.

"I'm still in my first trimester. It wouldn't take much." She ran a hand across her stomach.

"I'll be there for you," Michael said, sitting down on the bed next to her. "We're not ready for this. Someday, sure." He put a hand on her leg. "Someday it might be great news. But when it happens like this, when it's out of control, it can wreck everything. I don't know about you, but I feel like some kind of hostage."

Something in those words, Michael wasn't certain what it was, made Angela angry. She threw his hand off of her leg and ran to the bathroom, slamming the door behind her. "I'll make the goddamn appointment!" she shouted, and locked the door.

"I'll take off of work," Michael said through the door. "I'll drive you."

Angela stayed in the bathroom for nearly three hours. Twice Michael stood outside the door and heard pages turning.

~

The following morning, after Michael left the apartment, Angela called her doctor and said she wanted to have an ultrasound. Her doctor was a friend, and tried to discourage her, but Angela insisted.

At eleven o'clock, Angela lay on her back, her blouse pulled up and tucked beneath her breasts, her soft, white stomach reflecting the light. Warm, green, fluorescent gel was squeezed from a tube to a spot just below her navel, and the ultrasound technician smoothed it with the bulbous end of a white plastic wand that looked like a roll-on deodorant stick. This wand was connected to a computer by a white rubber cord. The computer screen was a haze of static in the shape of an overturned funnel; Angela could see it only by raising her head and leaning slightly to the side. The technician swiveled the screen away so Angela could not see it.

"I want to see," Angela said.

"The lights glare at that angle," she answered. "I'll turn it back in a minute."

Angela watched the woman's face, felt the gel cooling on her stomach. Suddenly the woman held the wand still, moving only the top from side to side. She raised her eyebrows, then dropped them into a frown, her face a mask of concentration.

"What is it?" Angela asked. "Boy or girl?"

The woman shook her head but didn't take her eyes off the screen. "I don't know," she said. Still she concentrated, moving the top of the wand in a short, circular arc, pressing gently into Angela's flesh.

"Is something wrong?" Angela asked. "Do I have a tumor or something?"

The woman didn't answer.

~

"And so I asked her again," Angela said to Michael that evening. "I said, 'Is it a tumor? Or what?' 'Twins,' she said, and smiled. 'You have twins.'"

"What?" Michael said.

"I know. I couldn't believe it either. She swung the screen around and there they were, little hearts throbbing, from head to toe no longer than my thumb."

"Twins," said Michael.

"Quite a shock, huh? I know this is not what you want to hear. But two I can't do, Michael. Two changes everything."

"Why did you even do this thing, Angela? You knew it would make it harder. You knew that."

Angela looked past the question.

"My doctor said it happens, sometimes, that during a second trimester procedure, an abortion, they find something like this. She said you have to verify the tissue, you know, count the parts, to make sure it's all out, so there won't be an infection later. Sometimes they count four legs and four arms. They never tell the woman. It's hard enough for her as it is."

Michael shook his head. "What are they? Boys? Girls?"

"Too soon to tell," Angela said.

"Too soon is right," Michael answered. "I mean, what am I supposed to do? What I want doesn't even matter here, Angela."

"It does matter," Angela said, "but I can't help it. I just can't do it. I don't expect anything from you. If you don't stay around, you don't." She smiled, and even laughed a little. "The nurse said it's a hell of a price to pay for seven inches of flesh and couple minutes of friction."

Michael managed a short laugh. "She got that right," he said.

～

Michael stayed, but he became preoccupied with thoughts of leaving. He could not get Angela to understand that his own feelings had not changed. There were so many things they could have done together. Mere seconds of physical pleasure had initiated a sequence of ritual action and conversation he could not overcome. His parents needed to be told, of course. They would expect a marriage, if not before the children arrived, then certainly after. This did not make him feel any better.

He began to page through the "For Rent" columns in the newspaper. He did this absent-mindedly. He was not seriously considering moving out, but he thought about it, fantasized about it. He knew it wouldn't end anything, that some things go on whether you are present or not. He remembered how excited he and Angela had been when they found the apartment they now shared, how they had stayed up until four in the morning eating pizza, drinking beer, and putting shelf paper in the kitchen cabinets. They had made love right on the kitchen floor, with boxes of dishes and pots and pans stacked all around them. Afterward, Angela had put a condom on the top of a beer bottle, held her thumb over it, and shook it up. The foam exploded and the rubber expanded like a balloon. It was a trick she had learned in her sorority, on "Safe Sex Night."

∼

The Eclipse. Any Excuse For a Party.

In July, Michael and Angela went to a party hosted by Olivia and John, who lived in a high-rise downtown. They had acquired permission from the manager to hold a party on the roof of their building to celebrate the partial solar eclipse. It was a classic Olivia and John affair. They made party tapes of songs with "sun" or "sunshine" in the title—Tape One, Side A: Stevie Wonder's "You Are the Sunshine of My Life;" Donovan's "Sunshine Superman;" The Beatles' "Here Comes the Sun;" Bill Withers' "Ain't No Sunshine When She's Gone;" James Taylor's "Sunny Skies;" and Gordon Lightfoot's "Sundown." They passed out large, thick pieces of colored glass, in red and green, through which one could safely look at the sun; they served Tequila Sunrises to everyone; they dressed in yellow, and encouraged everyone else to do the same.

About an hour before the eclipse, Angela tapped an empty glass with the blade of a butter knife. Michael stood by watching. This was a surprise.

"Everybody," Angela said. "I have an announcement to make."

The guests stopped talking and stared at her.

Angela flung open her arms. She was wearing an oversized yellow sundress, and it billowed in the breeze. "I'm pregnant," she said. "And it's twins."

"Twins!" Olivia said, rushing across the roof to hug Angela, her right hand steadying a drink.

Angela smiled as all the guests at the party, most of them friends of hers or Michael's, clapped and whistled.

Michael found himself shaking hands, smiling, accepting hearty slaps on the back. "A double-barreled penis," someone said, "way to go, stud." "One for each tit," said another, "no room for you." "Twin peaks," a third said. Michael laughed with them, but felt a ball of heat growing deep in his stomach.

John waited until the others had cleared away. "Twins!" he said to Michael. "Quite a surprise."

"Surprise about sums it up," Michael answered.

"I know this sounds like Mr. Moral Majority, but are you going to get married?"

Michael looked at John and shrugged. "I don't know what we're going to do."

Soon Olivia was walking around with a box full of colored glass. "Take one! Hurry! It's only a couple minutes away." Michael grabbed a piece of green glass, carefully avoiding the sharp edges. It was a shard from the thick bottom of a wine bottle. Angela came to him with a piece of red glass held over one eye.

"You look all Christmas-y," she said.

"Here it comes," John shouted. He was reclined in a lawn chair on his back, wearing welding glasses, which made him look like Darth Vader.

Michael put the glass to his eye and looked at the sun. Through the glass, it was a perfect white circle, its edges as sharp and clean as the blade of a knife. Along the bottom, a dark oval began to appear, moving imperceptibly across the sun. Next to him, Angela stared through the red glass, her head tipped so that her hair reached nearly to the small of her back. She grabbed Michael's free hand, squeezed it, and let it go.

"It looks like an oil spill," someone said.

"A penny on a plate."

"One of those little eyes they glue on stuffed animals. The ones that click and roll around."

It took nearly an hour for the moon to pass completely through the sun. The skies darkened only a little, and gradually most of the guests at the party lowered their eyes, rubbed their necks, and went back to their drinks. John rested with his hands behind his head and breathed the deep, shallow breaths of sleep.

Michael and Angela stood together, their faces parallel to the sky, the glass still covering their eyes. It was as if they were trying to outlast one another.

"What's it look like to you?" Angela asked.

"What's it look like to you?"

"Twins," Angela said. "It looks like twins."

"I don't know," Michael said. "It's too big and too far away to tell."

~

That night, they called their parents. They did it at the same time, on different phones. Michael and Angela each had separate lines and numbers. It was something they both had wanted when they moved in together.

When Michael hung up, Angela was already finished talking. Her parents lived in Chicago. Michael's were retired, and lived in Arizona.

"How'd it go?" Michael asked.

"Fine. Great," Angela said. "My parents were at Woodstock. They understand these things. They want to meet you. Yours?"

"They asked about marriage."

"What did they ask?"

"When," Michael said. "They wanted to know when."

"My dad wanted to know if," Angela said. "See. They're not so different. We did okay."

"Big difference between if and when," Michael said. "*We* haven't even talked about it."

"Well, we're living these lives, not them," Angela said. "It's 1992."

Michael wanted to ask what she meant by stating the year, as if it proved something, as if it provided a source of comfort. But he did not.

"My mom asked if we loved each other," Michael said.

"So did mine!" Angela said.

"What did you tell her?"

Angela shrugged. "I said, 'Isn't it obvious?' What did you say?"

"I said, 'Of course we do.' "This was exactly what he had said. But he had said it angrily, trying to sound insulted that the question was even asked. He was not convinced of his love for anyone just then.

Angela hugged him, locking her fingers around his waist. "God, this is still so unbelievable," she said. "You know, when I did the home test and found out, I visualized having my period. I used to sit and concentrate, trying to will the blood out of my body. I did sit-ups until I cried, it hurt so much. And then when I told you, and you said you didn't want it, like I knew you would, I could even feel that inside of me. It was like mentally we were banging on those kids, trying to knock them out of there, and they were hanging on for dear life." She smiled and looked up at him. "Strong little suckers."

"I'll say," Michael said.

They decided to get married privately, in the courthouse, after the babies arrived, so as not to appear to be bending to the pressure of public morality. They asked Olivia and John to be witnesses. They would invite their parents, too. In the meantime, they bought two cribs, two infant car seats, two of just about everything. They painted the second bedroom in their apartment, put up a teddy bear border around the top. And at night, Michael lay awake and lonely, listening to Angela breathe beside him, watching her stomach swell like the back of a white elephant.

∼

Late in September, Michael awoke to the sound of Angela moaning and getting sick in the bathroom. "Michael!" He sat up, disoriented, blinded by the sharp block of light from the bathroom. When he threw back the covers, his t-shirt suddenly felt wet and cold. It was five-thirty in the morning. Angela sat on the floor, her nightgown dark with blood. She was shivering.

"What's happening to me?" she screamed at him. Blood dried in dark lines in the creases of her hands.

Michael wrapped her in a blanket, carried her to the car, drove to the hospital.

Then he waited. A nurse told Michael this was very rare in the seventh month of pregnancy, but it sometimes happened. The doctor was performing an emergency C-section. The nurse would come by when she knew more.

She did not return for an hour and a half. In that time, two of the other men waiting in the room had been summoned to see their newborn children.

When the nurse returned, her lips were pursed. Michael stood up, and together they walked into the hall. "Angela's still a little groggy, but she's doing fine," she said. "She was carrying twins, a boy and a girl." The nurse put a hand on Michael's shoulder. He could feel the coolness of her fingertips through his shirt. "Your son seems to be doing okay. But we lost your little girl. I'm very sorry."

Michael felt sick to his stomach. He swallowed repeatedly to quench the burning in the back of his throat. "How could that happen?" he asked. "What happened?"

"She was stillborn. It's very hard, I know. But the poor thing didn't suffer. It really happens more than people think, but knowing that won't make you feel any better."

"But how? What could cause something like that?"

"Oh, it could be many things. The doctor will talk to you about it. She can answer your questions much better than I can. Your daughter wasn't as big as your son, who must have gotten most of the nutrition near the end. He'll be in NICU for a while, but he has a good chance." She smiled warmly and squeezed his arm. "If you come with me, you can see your wife."

Michael walked behind the nurse, squinting in the bright light of the hallway. He was very tired, and he blinked his eyes to try to clear them. When they reached the recovery room, the nurse sat Michael down in a chair outside.

"Now, you can sit here as long as you'd like. Your daughter is washed and wrapped in a blanket, and Angela is holding her. It's important for both of you to hold the baby, if you want to, touch her hair, call her by the name you picked out, whatever you'd like. This will be painful, but she's been part of your lives, especially Angela's, for seven months, and it's important for you to see her and to say goodbye."

Michael nodded. He took a deep breath and stood up. "I'm okay," he said. The nurse led him into the room.

Angela was lying on her back, her eyes closed. An I.V. dripped into her left arm. The room smelled of disinfectant. Her right arm encircled the infant. When Angela heard them, she opened her eyes and started to cry.

"Michael, I'm so sorry," she said. He kissed her on the open lips, which were dry and cracked from the anaesthesia.

"Hey, come on," he said. "You did fine. Let me see this little girl." Angela raised her arm and Michael picked the infant up. There was nothing to her. Her head, covered with wisps of dark hair, was not much larger than an orange. Even this small, the infant looked like Angela.

"Please," Angela said. "You can take it now."

"Okay, honey," the nurse said. She looked at Michael. He kissed the baby once, on the forehead, looked at the wrinkled face, then passed her awkwardly to the nurse. He put his hand over Angela's, but she was moaning quietly, falling asleep. Michael's hands were quivering. He could not hold them still.

"Morphine," the nurse said, to Michael. "She'll be very sleepy for awhile. You can stay with her as long as you'd like. Please come out to the nurse's station when you want to see your son."

~

That afternoon, Michael sat in sterile blue paper clothing watching a tiny, gray body writhe under a plexiglass dome. Round discs of white tape held blue and red wires to the infant's chest. A monitor beeped with each of the child's heartbeats, a muffled, electronic sound that increased when the infant moved and slowed when he was still. Michael reached a carefully scrubbed hand through a hole in the glass and ran his index finger back and forth along one of the little legs. The warm, wrinkled skin hung loosely on the bone.

A feeding tube curled into the infant's navel; a respirator taped to the mouth hissed every four seconds and made the ribs swell until the skin stretched over them tightly, like silk on a lampshade; the little hands opened and closed, with fingernails like the thin, opalescent scales of tropical fish. All together, two pounds, two ounces. A kilogram. A son.

Michael curled one arm awkwardly over the incubator. He pressed his forehead against the warm glass.

His eyes burned. But he could not look away.

Aliens

SO I HITCH a ride to Chicago with a guy driving pigs from Des Moines, a guy with one of those last name first names like Harrison or Starkey, who tells me, "Driving hogs ain't bad 'cause you're always upwind of the smelly little fuckers." That's the secret of life, he says. "Just stay upwind of all the shit." Like it's that easy, I'm thinking. Wind swirls around me like I'm the eye of a hurricane. He lets me off at O'Hare, drives his stinking rig right up to Arrivals and Departures, says, "watch them bastards hold their noses when I stop." I offer him the three crumpled dollars from my pocket, for gas, but he laughs and says the conversation was payment enough, which really is funny because he did all the talking. I just sat there all the way from Dubuque, trying to nod at the right times while not listening, which is an art, and wondering what part of a pig bacon comes from.

I'm holding those three dollars and my dad's American Express card when I walk into the lobby of the Airport Hilton. Thought ahead to make a reservation two weeks earlier from a pay phone at a Hardee's in Boulder, which was a good thing, the woman says now, because they're all booked up. "Smoking or non-smoking?" she asks, as she taps my name into the computer memory bank. They used to ask you that when you made plane reservations, but now they don't because they won't let anyone smoke on airplanes anymore.

"Non-smoking."

She taps her keyboard some more. "Sorry," she says. "Only smoking left."

"Does that mean I have to smoke?" It's a joke—I still have a sense of humor sometimes, even though my life is one tragically misunderstood episode after another. The woman clicks a perfectly-painted red fingernail on the faux-granite countertop and looks at me over her glasses. "I'll take it," I tell her.

"Two nights?" she asks.

"I'll be using it during the day, too, if that's all right." I hold out my father's American Express card. We have the same names, first and last, so I'm not worried about it.

I sign the slip, take the card back, and follow her directions to the elevator, holding a key that looks like a credit card with holes punched in it, like something you'd use to get from one chamber to another on the Starship Enterprise.

My hotel room is a fucking mansion, looks bigger than any trailer I ever lived in after I left my parents' house in Bloomington, Illinois. Now they have a condo in Florida, Heaven's Waiting Room, they call it, where there are more Cubans than in Cuba, where it's so hot sometimes cars sink right up to their axles in blacktop parking lots, and where alligators just ate some little boy out canoeing with his parents. "Visit us anytime," my dad says.

Anyway, my hotel room has two full size beds. A bathroom with a mirror the size of a garage door. Color T.V., cable, and pay-per-view. The card on top of the set features a roster of first-run Hollywood movies and, on the flip side, triple-X porn flicks. In the old days, when I was less in control of myself, I might have grabbed the box and watched everything, the Hollywood pics and the porn, one after the other, run up seventy-five or so dollars worth of marathon pay-per-viewing at seven-fifty a pop. But now I'm focused. I have a reason to live, as they say.

I take a shower, dry off, put on my clothes again, check to make sure I have the green charge card in my pocket, and go down to the lobby to find out where I'm supposed to go. As luck would have it, I walk right into a schedule board that lists everything going on. My convention group is meeting in the Illinois Room, on the sixth floor. Some kind of religious revival is also going on at the Civic Center downtown, which explains the unusually high number of people in wheelchairs with crosses hanging around their necks. Before, see, I would have spent the whole two days in my room watching television, wondering which of these events to go to, paralyzed by indecision. But now I have focus. It's amazing what focus will do for you. If I had the self-discipline, I would maybe write a book about it. Focus, I'd call it, and get stinking rich like all those other self-help charlatans who didn't do shit for me.

The convention room is nice, red carpet, a chandelier, white tablecloths on round tables. I get the day's program and my stick-on name tag at the door. Some hippie in a cowboy hat and a pony tail is up at the podium, a guy the program identifies as Dr. Tom Wadsworth, who is writing a book about how the government is hiding evidence of extraterrestrial visitation, including actual extraterrestrials frozen in liquid nitrogen, in some warehouse in Washington D.C., probably the same place the Smithsonian keeps all its extra Indian bones. I look around the room and see nobody laughing, so I figure I'm in the right place.

"The Sixth Annual Meeting of the E.T. Encounters Group" and "Welcome All" are written in red on two banners that hang above and behind the podium where the space cowboy is talking. I sit down at a table by myself and listen for awhile.

"Furthermore," the man says, "I have evidence proving that ex-president Bush met with extraterrestrials in the Arizona desert. Radar picked up three unidentified flying objects, moving at nearly the speed of light, which disappeared on or near a United States Army base. Ten minutes later, Air Force One made an unscheduled and unreported stop there. After Air Force One departed, which was approximately forty-five minutes later, the three unidentified flying objects flew away. This circumstantial evidence is supported by far more compelling testimony from two Navaho tribal police officers. I have sworn affidavits signed by these two officers, testifying that they witnessed George Bush shaking hands with a thin, silvery creature with a large, misshapen head. . . ."

I stop listening and scan my program. The event I'm interested in—the only reason I'm here—is scheduled for that evening, from seven p.m until midnight. It is titled, simply, "Encounter Testimony." The program includes directions explaining that any conventioneer interested in narrating his or her encounter with an extraterrestrial being would be permitted to do so at fifteen minute intervals throughout the evening. To do this, one merely has to sign up with the secretary. One also has to sign a release form, which would allow the organization to videotape your testimony for research purposes.

Nervously, I pick the eight-forty-five slot and initial the release form. A thirtyish woman with thick, pretty lips and dyed-blonde hair signs up after I do. I notice that she wears rings on all eight fingers and both thumbs, which, along with her earrings, represent all twelve signs of the zodiac. "Look forward to hearing you, darlin'," she says. She has a southern accent. "I go on at eight-thirty, right before you."

I smile and nod.

"You look nervous," she says. "Your first convention?"

"Yes."

"Welcome," she says, and takes my hand. With all those rings, it feels like I'm shaking hands with the bar of a chain saw. "Don't be nervous," she says. "These people have changed my life. There's a whole other world out there, and when thought I was the only one who knew about it, I almost killed myself." She turns her wrists up to show me her scars. "I was kidnapped from the parking lot of a Winn-Dixie in Birmingham, Alabama, manifested aboard a space ship and taken somewhere out there," she waved one hand at the ceiling, "and returned to my car, the exact same time, a week later. My husband left me. My kids are afraid to talk to me. No one, not even my minister, would believe me. But these people did. You can walk with your head high around here."

"I plan to," I tell her, sliding my hand free of all those rings.

"Well good," she says. "See you later, darlin'."

Seeing as it's four-thirty, and I haven't eaten since I left Dubuque that morning, I head to the hotel bar for some supper, and to think about what I'm going to say, and how I'm going to say it. I sit down with a pretzel basket, take out the charge card, and order a vodka on the rocks.

"Run a tab, sir?" the bartender asks, gripping my dad's charge card between his thumb and forefinger, like he's holding a butterfly gently by its wings. Sometimes at truck stops I'll walk along the front of those rumbling, smelly rigs, pulling butterflies from the grills, lifting their quivering wings right off the radiators. I might be in Colorado, somewhere, or

Ohio, and I'll wonder where the butterfly came from, wonder if it was just flitting happily across the blacktop in some Kansas prairie town when WHAM! it got sucked up by some hot steel monster and driven halfway across the country. Lots of times, though, and this is the most amazing part, I pull those damn butterflies alive from the grill, the orange ones with black dots, especially, put them down, and they'll kind of walk around for awhile in the oily gravel, opening and closing their ragged wings, and pretty soon they'll just up and fly away. Damned if that don't almost make me cry every time.

"Should I run a tab, sir?" the bartender asks again, more insistent.

"Please," I say.

I've had my dad's charge card about nine months now, since the aliens invaded my life. He came to meet me, right after it happened. Flew from Miami into Indianapolis, paid the cab fare to my place, or what used to be my place, before the aliens landed in my back yard. Come stay with us in Florida for awhile, he said. But what about the alligators, I said. And the hurricanes. Look at what Andrew did. And what about Castro, Dad? You can practically skip a stone from Miami to Cuba. No, I think I'll stick around here. I'll be fine. Really. If not, I'll move around.

So he gave me a hug and disappeared. But he left that little green American Express card sitting on my steps, a card with his name—and mine—printed on the front, in little raised letters, like braille. On the back, above that brownish magnetic stripe, was a little piece of masking tape, with Dad's phone number written on it. I took the number off and taped it inside of my shoe.

Before he retired, my dad used to be an airline pilot, so it's not like he can't afford to make the payments. I'm frugal, too. Anyway, he hasn't cancelled the card yet, so he must be all right with my quest, with what I'm doing. He had one lung removed about a month ago, needed some radiation, but I guess he's breathing well enough with the lung they left in.

I order another basket of pretzels and another vodka, and then another. I lose count at five or six, because I'm thinking about my speech, and before I know it, it's eight-thirty.

I get back to the sixth floor just in time to see the blonde with the rings finish up her story. I can't make much sense of it, to tell you the truth, but

I notice she has decent legs when she's standing up there, something I hadn't noticed before.

After she's finished, and everyone claps for her, she returns to her chair at a table. She gives me a thumbs up as she passes me, and I see that the ring on her thumb has a ram's head on it. Then a man calls my name, and I wander onto the platform and stand in a spotlight in front of the microphone while the man adjusts it up to my mouth. I tap the mike twice with my finger, say "testing," and get started. Straight ahead of me, a fat bald man is crouched behind a videocamera mounted on a silver tripod. When I start talking, a little red light comes on inside the camera, and the bald man sits down.

"I'm happy to be here to tell you my story," I say, beginning with the lines I'd rehearsed in the bar downstairs. "Since the aliens invaded my life, I have been living from one nightmare to the next, hoping it was all a dream, that I would wake up and everything would be the way it was before. But I know that won't happen now. I don't know what I did to deserve this, but hell, I know, as I'm sure you all do, that life isn't fair.

"I wasn't around when they came the first time, when they took my wife. I was out, gone somewhere, I don't remember. But I came home, like I always did, and she was gone. Vanished without a trace. It was about three o'clock in the morning, and it was as if she just merged with the air. All her stuff was still there. The last cigarette she smoked was still in the ashtray. The only thing missing, other than her, was her purse. I believe in my heart that the aliens came and took her away, and swear to God, I have not heard from her since.

"But that time, they left me my little girl. I walked into her bedroom, and she was laying there sleeping, my little angel, six years old and innocent of all the shit that happens in the world. In the morning, she asked me where her mother was, and I told her I didn't know, which is what I thought then. But like I said, I know now what happened.

"I admit, I didn't handle it as well as I should have. I mean, when aliens come in and fuck up your life, it's not as if they give you some practice dealing with it. I spent more time away from my little girl than I should have, maybe a week or two at the longest stretches, looking for my wife, or just living, you know. I figured my girl was big enough to take care of herself. She could answer the phone. She could wash her clothes in the sink. She could cook, you know. I told her while I was gone she didn't have to go to school.

"I don't know how much time went by, but one day, I came home, and there was an alien there waiting for me, disguised as a man in a suit, and he told me my little girl was gone somewhere being raised for the time being by people who smile far too often, people who watch public television, people who can buy my little girl a bigger bicycle each year, when her legs grow longer.

"But you see, as much as I try to believe that, I know it's not true. Because when I got a drink and went out back, there were four burnt spots in the yard, spots the size of dinner plates, black as coal, where they landed in their little spaceship."

The bald man stands up by the videocamera, and I see the red light inside go off. This throws my concentration for a second, makes me forget what I'm talking about. But I take a drink of water and recover.

"It's like the man earlier this afternoon, the guy in the cowboy hat, said, it's a government conspiracy to keep it all covered up, keep it all secret. I just know it is. I call the government up on the telephone, tell them I want my little girl back, and they pretend they don't know me. They say, 'Who is this?' I even tried the White House once, called President Clinton, figured he's a Democrat maybe he'll listen, but some woman—maybe it was Hillary, I don't know—answered, and wouldn't put me through.

"So now I'm trying to find my daughter on my own. I thought maybe some of you people could help me. Maybe when they came for you, they took you someplace and you saw my little girl. I have a picture of her in my pocket if you want to check. I'm in room 302. Stop by if you think you've seen her. She's seven now, but I'm sure unless they cut her hair she still looks pretty much the same. But I'm thinking maybe the aliens brought her back, maybe they dropped her off someplace and she can't find her way home. Maybe she's like that girl in the Wizard of Oz wandering around, looking for me."

When I finish, people just keep staring at me, like they expect me to say more. A few people clap a little bit, but it doesn't catch on. Most of the people are quiet, stunned is what I'm thinking. The man who introduced me smiles and waves his arm toward the side of the stage, where I'm supposed to leave, so I walk that way, hoping that I made some sense, because I know that sometimes after a vodka or two I don't make as much sense to others as I make to myself. I walk down off the platform. The old woman on her way up, the speaker following me, smiles and pats my arm gently as we pass on the stairs.

Though it's only about nine o'clock, I'm tired, and I decide to go back to my room. I feel happy that I've accomplished what I set out to do, and think maybe I'll watch a movie and have a drink or two to wind down, to celebrate. Midway through "Unforgiven," just after Gene Hackman whips Clint Eastwood's buddy to death, somebody knocks on my door.

It would have been sweet, wouldn't it, movie-of-the-week, stringed orchestra shit, if it had been my little girl on the other side of that door. But when I open it, the blonde woman from the E.T. convention, the one from Alabama with all the zodiac rings on her fingers, is standing there. She has a silver ice bucket with a green bottle of champagne poking out the top, two champagne glasses sticking out of her fingers, and she smiles at me with those thick lips and says, "Hey darlin', can I come in for a minute?" Which, translated, means, I'm coming in and I'm staying a lot longer than that. I cast one final, forlorn look at Clint Eastwood on the T.V. screen, figuring I only got half my seven-fifty worth of that movie, and let her in.

We turn off the T.V., sit down on the end of the bed, and make small talk for about an hour while we drink the champagne. We talk about anything that comes to our minds, cover a lot of subjects, so I have the chance to ask her if she knows what part of a pig bacon comes from. She says, "From the back, darlin'." Then she grabs my hand and says, "I have to tell you the truth. I lied to you downstairs. Aliens never kidnapped me in no Winn-Dixie parking lot in Birmingham."

"They didn't?" I try to sound shocked.

She shakes her head. "No," she says, "they didn't. There was a bag boy there, nineteen years old, looked just like Mel Gibson the actor, only taller. Every Saturday for about six months, he'd wheel my groceries out to the car, put them in the trunk for me, and I'd watch him while he bent over the back of my car, looking at his blue jeans, the little worn circle on one back pocket where he kept his dippin' tobacco. And that one Saturday, he said, 'I got a new motorcycle yesterday.'

" 'What kind?' " I asked.

" 'Harley Davidson,' he said. 'You want a ride?' "

"I don't know what happened. The way I see it, everybody in this world has one moment in their life when all their stars line up in one, spontaneous chorus line, when they have to take a chance and forget the consequences. I tucked my purse under my arm and off we went. We drove about fifty miles straight south on I-65, eighty miles an hour, the wind blowing my hair back, my fingers digging into the muscular spaces between his ribs. We stopped at an Econo-Lodge, charged a room on my husband's Visa, and I spent one glorious week eating McDonald's hamburgers twice a day and making love to the most beautiful young man I have ever seen."

She looks at me and takes a drink of champagne. I pick up the bottle to pour her some more, but it's gone.

"What about you, darlin'?" she asks, rubbing the palm of my hand with one of her fingers, like she's about to tell my fortune. "Aliens *really* fly off with your wife and child?"

With my free hand, I lift some of her hair over one of her ears. She has thick, detached lobes, and on that particular ear there is a large, red earring in the shape of a crab—the sign for Cancer. I kiss her neck. "Yes they did," I say. "All I know is what I know. First one, and then the other."

"Darlin' I believe you," she says. "Everybody's got to have faith in something." With one hand, she unbuttons my pants and relieves the pressure. She reaches down inside my underwear, grabs my standard transmission, and starts up and down with her hand, with all those sharp rings on her fingers, and I have this nightmare vision of someone peeling a carrot with one of those potato peelers, but it passes.

When we're naked, she keeps saying, "I'm your vehicle baby, I'll take you anywhere you want to go," which, if I remember right, is a line from a '60s song by a band called the Ides of March.

～

When I wake up at four in the morning, all that digested champagne and vodka sloshing around in my bladder, the woman is gone. I walk naked into the bathroom in the dark, feel for the toilet bowl with my shins. When I finish, I go back into the room, sit down on the end of the bed, and turn on the television. I have to squint my eyes at first because the screen is so bright. The twenty-four-hour weather channel comes on, a radar screen with one thin line, like the hand of a clock, circling, with Chicago in the middle. Each time the line passes over the screen, lime green clouds appear, like electric Rorschach splotches.

I pick up my clothes, which are scattered on the floor, and of course when I check my pockets for the American Express card, it's gone. But at least this time I know it was stolen by someone with flesh and blood, someone human. And she left me the three dollars, which I find pressed flat under the empty champagne bottle, with that little earring shaped like a crab right next to them—probably an omen of some kind.

So I get dressed, except for my socks and shoes, and watch the weather channel until the sun comes up. I get to thinking for awhile that maybe aliens even control the weather. Shit happens—floods, hurricanes, tornados, earthquakes, hail the size of apples or whatever—and we aren't doing it to ourselves, right? Think about it.

But when the light comes streaming through the cracks in the curtains, I get focused again. Every few minutes, an airplane roars past outside, coming or going, and the rumbling clears my head.

I have to make some decisions. I know that now. I still have my safety valve, that size ten shoe with my dad's phone number taped inside. But I keep wondering what would be more suicidal: to try to keep living the life I'm living, or make that collect telephone call to Florida, take my chances with the alligators, face down Castro, knowing that any day a wind with a name might come out of the sky and blow us all away.

The Blue Heron

ONE WINTER NIGHT, while bent over the stove, making gravy, my mother flowed peacefully down the cabinets like a little waterfall and puddled on the dirty kitchen floor.

"That happens the moment your soul leaves you," Father said later, to console me. "A bird flies into a window, it's the same thing. The soul passes through to the next world, but the body drops like a feathered bag of water."

Mother had burst an aneurysm in her head while stirring cornstarch into chicken boullion. The sudden silence startled us, made us feel as if all the air had been sucked from the house. If she'd died as she'd lived, Mother's last breath should have been a roar.

In a small town, news of a death spreads door to door with the morning mail. Word of Mother's death spread even more quickly than usual because no one liked her. People in town found her loud and stubborn (she was both), and everyone—other women, especially—thought she mistreated Father. "Poor Henry," they'd say. "She won't even let him have a dog." I'd see them pointing and whispering in church, or while we were grocery shopping. "Here comes Amy Maddox," they'd say, and they'd cover their children's ears with their hands. One thing they said was indisputable. Sometimes when Mother yelled, you felt like you had steel ball bearings rattling around in your ears.

Mother's death set off a muted celebration in town. Even before the obituary came out in the local newspaper, food started appearing on our porch—platters of beef and pork roast, steaming casseroles and sweet-smelling breads, pies, plates of cookies, bottles of milk. After eating our fill, my father and I would put the empty plates and bowls and pans back on the porch, unwashed. Two men so long under the influence of that woman wouldn't know better, the neighbors must have thought, heartened by our appetites, and charmed by our lack of good manners.

The day after Mother died, Dad started building a cedar fence eight feet high all around the yard with a gate across the driveway for his pickup truck to pass through. I helped him by digging the post holes every eight feet by hand after thawing the frozen ground with charcoal. "Out in the country, they dig graves in the winter this way," Dad said, as we listened to the earth hissing under each little mound of smoking briquets. Many days, he kept me home from school to dig those holes. By March the fence was done.

People in town didn't know what to think. Some said Dad was so happy his wife died that he danced all night in the yard and didn't want the neighbors to see him. Others said he was so distraught he went crazy. I couldn't tell who was right.

Without Mother there to filter his ideas for him, separate the grit from the gold, keep him from running off, as she'd say, "with one of your three-quarters fried, half-baked, quarter-boiled stupid ideas like filling half of the basement with dirt and turning it into a worm farm or raising rainbow trout in a swimming pool," Dad discovered he could do anything he wanted. "A single man dreams dreams a married man can only dream about," he used to say to me at dinner, while Mother shouted down one foolish idea after another. Once Dad wanted to buy a hot air balloon and keep it moored in the backyard. Another time he wanted to buy some land and raise elk because their shed antlers were worth money in the Orient.

"Don't marry a dreamer," Mother would say to me. "It's like buying a mule that wants to fly. Hook him up to your cart and he'll just stand there, waiting for wings."

"I'm the man of your dreams, Amy," Father would say, the argument lost, grabbing her around the waist with one thick arm to pull her on his lap.

"If this is a dream, somebody wake me up," Mother would answer.

Then they would smile at one another and laugh—loud, wheezing, snorting laughter that would end, usually, with a kiss. It puzzled me how they went from shouting at one another to laughing together as if it were natural, like rolling down a hill.

After Mother died, the sudden quiet was hard on both Dad and me. We built the fence in silence, but I could feel Dad's ideas changing the air pressure. It seemed like each time he tamped in another fence post, he dumped another bag of sand that held down his helium-filled head. With only me left trying to keep his feet on the ground, Dad floated away.

~

It started with one female calf that a farmer delivered to us in the back of his pick-up truck.

"You're in the middle of the flippin' city!" the farmer said, astonished, when he stepped down from his truck. "You've got sidewalks and everything!"

The farmer had tobacco spit in his beard and was skinny as a weathered scarecrow. No match for Henry Maddox, certainly, who was tall and barrel-chested, built like a hairy zeppelin.

"I got a fourth of an acre here," Dad said, defensively. "I'll put in alfalfa, grow some corn and some soybeans. Hell, it's just one little cow."

"But look here," the farmer interceded. "You can't raise a calf here. There's zoning laws. This here's R1 or R2. You need Ag for raising beef cattle. Buy yourself a forty or two, do it right."

"Can't," Dad said. "My wife died in this house. Are you going to sell me the cow or not?"

"Sorry about the wife," the farmer said, and spat in the grass. "Heard she yelled a lot."

"Thank you," my dad said. "She did."

The farmer left us the calf.

We named her "Dinner," and when she grew so big she started denting the car and the aluminum siding, punching her heavy head through the first-floor window screens, Dad decided she was ready for the freezer. While I distracted her with a carrot, my father thumped her on the skull just above her eyes with a sledgehammer, and Dinner dropped like a pile of topsoil. Even with Dad's bandsaw set up in the garage, it took us two days to cut her up. Our feet stuck to the blood congealed and blackened on the floor. It took us five days to wash it from our hair and from the whorls of our fingerprints. We doused the offal—four wheelbarrows full—with gasoline, and burned them late at night, in the garden, so neighbors wouldn't see the smoke.

After that, Dad said he wouldn't raise beef cattle anymore. "Too damn messy," he said. "I have a better idea."

He was gone for three days.

When he returned, the bed of his pick-up sagged under the weight. Curled in the back, a pillowcase tied around her head, her feathered body netted like a sack of store potatoes, her powerful legs bound together with about two-hundred feet of nylon rope, was an ostrich nine feet tall.

"Isn't she something?" Dad said, slapping my back. "Got legs as strong as a horse and wings like a penguin."

"Where'd you find her?" I asked.

"Oklahoma," he said. "Game farm down there got just about everything. Cost fourteen hundred dollars." He smiled and winked. "All my savings."

We set the ostrich free in the garage. I held her head with my hands over her eyes while my father cut the rope from her legs. She leaped immediately to her feet, looked around in a daze, and then exploded. We crouched in one corner, holding a garden rake and a broom to protect ourselves as she ran hysterically from one end of the garage to the other, thumping her head on each of the overhead rafters, solid two by eight wooden beams, as she passed. She left smears of blood on the wood each time she struck her head.

Dad said, "I've got an idea works with bees. Get one in the house at night, all you got to do is turn out the lights. It'll fall just like a snowflake."

So he worked his way along the wall to a light switch and turned off the lights.

The ostrich stopped running, but pranced around the garage nervously, her toenails clicking on the concrete. Blood dripped from the holes in her beak to the floor.

"Save up to buy a male," Dad said, "throw some straw around in here, maybe paint an African scene on the back of the garage door to make them comfortable, and before you know it we'll have eggs the size of basketballs for breakfast, shells so hard we'll have to crack them with a hammer." He looked at me. "What do you think of that?"

The next morning, we found the ostrich dead, her head a bloody pulp of flesh and feathers, her neck stiff as a cane.

"Son of a bitch," Dad said, when he saw her. He slumped to the floor.

"She was too tall," I said.

He stared at the ostrich for a long while, ran a hand through the black feathers on her belly. Then he chuckled quietly. He looked up at me. "Can you *imagine* the look on your mother's face, seeing this in here?"

I smiled.

"Boy oh boy," he said, "Ain't many women in the world could yell like Amy. She had a throat like a bagpipe."

~

Though the death of his ostrich tempered Dad's enthusiasm for large, exotic animals, it made him all the more determined to bring smaller animals home and keep them alive. In the end, he was marching them in two by two. It was as if he had one eye trained on the sky, waiting for the flood.

He found the animals all over. Some, he live-trapped; others, he bought from game farms and petting zoos; he sent away air-express for a few. We soon owned a pair of red foxes, which stayed in a pen he built behind the house; three ring-necked pheasants, wings clipped, who ran free and kept the foxes salivating and snapping their jaws like traps; a half-dozen chickens and one noisy rooster; four prairie dogs which dug up the yard like giant moles; a billy goat; a pair of noisy peacocks; a ferret, which stayed in the house most of the time; and a baby llama, which also roamed the yard freely but slept in the garage on an old, twin-bed mattress.

The animals kept coming, too. I couldn't tell if he wanted me to stop him. Dad couldn't stop himself. He didn't know how. But he tried, once.

Sometime after school let out for the summer, in early June, Dad put down the paper one evening and looked at me. He'd been unusually quiet for a few days, so I knew something was on his mind. "It's been six months," he said. "I've had my eye on this woman at the grocery store, about my age, left us apple pie every week back when your mama died. Remember that pie?"

I nodded.

"Was good, wasn't it?" he said. "Just the right amount of cinnamon. Should I ask her over, so we can meet her?"

"Sure," I said. "If you want."

"I don't know if she's the right kind of woman," he said. "But you can't find out if you just smile at her when she rings up your bologna. Right?"

"Right Dad," I said.

She came over on a Saturday and she seemed very nice. Her name was Mary. She was a small bowling ball of a woman who had a nervous habit of running her index finger over the furniture, checking for dust. My father fixed a beef roast and still chuckled when he called "Dinner!" even though the joke was old by now.

The early afternoon passed pleasantly. Then, while we were eating, Dad's ferret wandered into the kitchen, looking like somebody's stuffed gray stocking, nosed around our feet, then stuck his head up the leg of Mary's pants.

We looked under the table at the same time. Dad looked at me and smiled. Instinctively, with happy anticipation, we put our hands to our ears.

Encouraged by the traction he could get on Mary's pantyhose, the ferret climbed her leg, up the narrowing tunnel of her pants, squeezing past her knee and then groaning as he struggled over her thigh and nestled into her crotch.

Mary smiled politely, wiped her mouth with her napkin, and stood up. Calmly, she turned her back to the table, undid her pants, and pulled the ferret out, holding it under her arm as she rezipped.

"What a funny little animal!" she exclaimed, sitting down again. "What do you call him?"

"It's a ferret," Dad answered. He looked so disappointed I thought he was going to cry.

Mary placed the ferret on the table next to her plate, and scraped some of the beef to the side for him to eat. "The poor thing is starving," Mary said.

Dad escorted Mary from the house without even serving dessert.

He stopped going to work after that. He stopped washing, stopped changing his clothes, even. He spent nearly all his time with the animals.

The yard began to smell, too. I'm sure our neighbors must have noticed it much sooner than I did, but because we'd suffered a death in the family, they were granting us more courtesy than expected, even in a small town. One afternoon, I'd walked downtown to buy some groceries, and when I returned, as I approached the gate, I could smell that pungent, earthy odor from over a block away. Even more shocking to me was the cacophony of animal sounds coming from our yard. Surely, I thought, as I locked the driveway gate behind me, people could *hear* what was going on. Surely, they could *smell* it.

Inside the house, I found Dad in the kitchen. A blue heron was standing in the stainless steel sink. Goldfish were swimming in the water at its feet.

"Look what I found," Dad said. "Out by the lake. Some of his wing feathers are crimped, but the bones seem okay. I think he was hit by a car."

"Dad," I said.

"Looks like a giant bluejay, doesn't he?" my father laughed. "Those long legs bend backwards at the knee, not like ours."

"Dad," I said, "we have to talk."

"So talk," he said. But when I mentioned the smells and the noise, he seemed unconcerned.

"Ah, hell," he said, waving his hand at me. "We've got a few little animals, big deal. All together, they're still quieter than one miserable barking dog."

"It's *not* just a few," I said. "I counted. We have thirty-seven. Thirty-eight now, counting the heron."

"Well," he said, defensively, "herons don't make any noise at all, far as I can tell."

"But what about the smell?" I said. "It smells like shit out there. In here, too."

Dad said, "It smells like nature." He took a deep breath, and then exhaled. "If a guy could bottle that air and sell it in the cities, he'd be a millionaire. Maybe we should think about doing that, you and me. Call it Farm Fresh Air, something like that."

Then I went too far. "You smell too, Dad," I said.

He stared at me, his eyes like two pennies glowing at the bottom of a well. "Get out of this house," he said. But he shouted after me, as I ran out the door, "Be back before dark."

∼

The next afternoon, as if to rebuke me further, my father brought home two otters, four bobwhite quail, and a cage full of blue and green parakeets. He let the parakeets go free inside of the house. One of them flew up the stairs to the second floor. The others flitted around the kitchen, their wings dusting the ceiling and cabinets.

"Watch this," he said, putting a small dab of peanut butter on his head. One by one, the parakeets alighted in his hair, and Dad smiled like a king wearing a colorful, feathered crown.

"Dad," I said.

"What?" His eyes stared up, trying to see the birds in his hair, pecking at the peanut butter.

"Nothing," I said.

"Here," he said, holding out the jar of peanut butter. "You try it."

I left the house and walked downtown until dark. I knew that what we had living in the yard would make the newspapers, that it would go out on the wire services like stories of old women who secretly harbor four hundred cats in their basement, or old men who keep baby alligators in their bathtubs until they're too big, and they end up mysterious monsters haunting golf course water hazards and county park ponds.

So I did what I had to do. Half of my blood was my mother's after all.

∼

I arranged to be away the next morning and much of the afternoon, and figured by three o'clock, when I got back home, it would all be over. But when I walked around the corner, I saw a small crowd of people gathered in the street in front of our house. Two police cars, their blue and red lights flashing, were on the other side of the street at the curb. Parked behind them was a truck full of empty cages with the words, "Waushara County Animal Welfare" stenciled on the side.

"You the one that called?" the tallest policeman asked.

I nodded.

"You did the right thing, son," he said.

"What's going on?" I asked.

He looked up at the house, the second floor looming above the cedar fence. The gate across the driveway was closed.

"Your pa went a little crazy," the other officer said. "He ordered us off the property. When we were leaving to get a warrant, we backed over one of his woodchucks."

"Those are prairie dogs," I said.

"Whatever. And your pa just went berserk. He's got all the animals in the house with him, and he's barricaded the doors and the gate." He pointed up at Dad's bedroom. One of the windows was open. "He's got a BB gun or a pellet gun or something. He's already cracked the windshield of one of the patrol cars."

"He hasn't shot at any people," the other officer said. "Just the vehicles. We've got someone from Human Services coming out to talk to him, but she can't get here for awhile."

The eerie, muffled call of a peacock echoed from somewhere inside the house.

"Lookit there!" somebody said, pointing. The llama walked lazily passed the open window, pausing to look outside at the flashing lights before disappearing again.

"Jesus," someone said. "That was a horse or something. He's got a horse in there with him."

One of the green parakeets flitted out the window and landed in a maple tree near the street.

"Look out, here he comes!" somebody shouted. Suddenly my father, Noah the terrorist in his land-locked ark, appeared at the window, my BB gun at his shoulder. Everybody dropped to the ground except the police officers and me. I heard the snap of the trigger, and a second later the BB bounced off the driver's side window of the second patrol car, leaving a small spider web of cracks.

"Watch where you're aiming that goddamn thing!" someone shouted from his knees, waving a fist in the air.

Dad disappeared again.

"Do something, Jerry!" the man yelled at one of the police officers. "Tear gas the bastard!"

If the man had been closer, I would have kicked him.

A flurry of noise on the roof attracted our attention again. Dad's billy goat had his front legs out the window. His belly was caught on the sill, and he grunted as he scrambled to lift his hind quarters through. A blue parakeet stood on his back and pecked at the lice in his fur. Once out of the bedroom and safely on the roof, the goat scampered around the dormer and up to the peak, near the chimney. The parakeet flew off.

"Lookit that, now!" someone said. "He's got animals on his god-damn roof! That's got to be against the law!"

The tall policeman looked at his partner. "What do you think?" he asked. "We could call the fire department, get their ladder truck out here." The other officer shrugged.

The llama stepped through the window to the roof, sure-footed and calm, to join the billy goat.

And then, as if it were consciously asserting its clumsy grace at the peak moment of our chaos, the blue heron stepped to the window, hopped up on the sill, and looked down at us, his black pupils set in round, golden eyes, like embryos curled in egg yolks.

Everyone stood up. "What in the hell is that thing?" someone asked.

"A great blue heron," the animal welfare officer answered. He had one hand in a salute against his forehead, shading his eyes. "What a beautiful bird," he said.

Without ceremony, the heron coiled his neck, spread his damaged wings, and leaped from the windowsill. We watched as he glided toward us, tipping unsteadily, from side to side, his wings waggling as they cupped the air, his neck crooked like the trap in the drain plumbing beneath a sink.

"That thing can barely fly," a policeman said.

"He ain't gonna clear the fence," someone said. "He's gonna hit the fence. Watch out!"

But the heron glided over Dad's fence and soared magnificently over our heads, bathing us in his shadow, his feet and legs extended stiffly behind him. With wings spread, he looked bigger and heavier than he was, and I could see that even though he cleared the fence, his angle of descent was too steep. He began to flap as he passed over us, across the street, toward a row of houses, losing altitude rapidly. His feet skimmed the roof of a patrol car, and though he twisted and banked to avoid the collision, he slammed hard into one of the houses. The sound of his body thumping against the wood echoed down the street.

Someone said, "He broke his neck."

For a moment, the heron didn't move. I looked up and saw Dad watching from the window. The ferret was on his shoulder, poking its nose under the collar of his shirt. Dad waved, but he looked like a stranger.

Slowly, the heron stirred. He raised himself on spindly legs like a flag, then paused, as if to consider his possibilities.

"He's okay!" someone shouted. "Hey look!"

Once more, the heron dropped his beak, coiled his neck, spread his wings, and jumped. With a fury of noisy flapping, he headed back towards us. He landed first on the police car, sliding across the hood as if it were glazed with ice, then leaped again, passing over our heads and up toward the house, climbing, banking left, then right, past the startled billy goat and the cloud-white llama, over the rooftop, then out over the city and out of sight.

I looked up at my father. He stood on the roof now, and you could see even from the ground that his clothes were rotting off him. Like the rest of us, he had watched the heron disappear. He looked confused, sad.

"You old enough to take care of yourself for awhile, son?" one of the police officers asked me, quietly. "Someone nearby you can stay with, for awhile?"

I ignored him. I was staring at my father, who was looking up at the sky. I don't know how I know, but I'm certain he was thinking about Mother—his wife, Amy—and how she would have yelled and carried on to prevent this whole spectacle. I looked at Dad's billy goat wandering on our rooftop, nibbling at the shingles curled by the summer heat. For the first time, I sensed how little I or anyone knew of what my parents had meant to one another. We all read the world with our own eyes, I know that, but I began to understand that what others had mistaken for a bad marriage was actually one of the truest kinds of married love, the kind that filled genuine need, knowing it would sometimes be loud and messy, knowing, especially, that it would cost miracles.

Secrets Men Keep

I HAVE A FRIEND named Mavis who believes it isn't easy being a white man in the 1990s. The glory days are over, he says. We are the last generation of a dying breed, men who put vitamin-enriched white bread on every table, sent men to the moon, created a system of mass production that put an average of 2.2 color televisions in every home in America. Now all these other guys—your Blacks, your Hispanics, your Asians, your Indians, you name it, have said wait a minute, you stepped on us on your way up the ladder, now we're going to step on you.

Not to mention women, I tell him, because I know his views on that subject.

He says, Don't get me started. Look at Kennedy, he says. That charisma couldn't happen today. Why? Because he's a rich, white s.o.b. and the press would sniff out every little thing he ever did, would stick their carrot-long noses up his asshole until he breathed Vitamin A. Used to be a man could carry his secrets with dignity. Used to be all that mattered were the products of his genius. So he told a Black joke in the commissary—he just kicked Hitler's ass up to his eyeballs! So he rubbed up against his secretary's backside in the elevator—he just erected the Hoover Dam, stopped up a whole goddamn river! Indians had this country for thousands of years and did they ever build so much as one dam? Hell no!

Mavis and I are sitting in The Sports Bar having a beer, and I'm tape recording everything he says because I'm writing a book about American men and he's agreed to be in it. I don't know what kind of book it will be, but I want to call it *Just Men*, or something like that. My agent says a title such as *American Apollos* would have enormous marketing potential; he sees a spin-off television series and perhaps even a men's cologne of the same name. He's very excited about this project. Everyone I talk to about the book suggests a different title. Today the bartender, a man named Steve who's also in the book, had another suggestion: *Fears, Cheers, Beers, and No Queers.* Catchy, I told him, but inaccurate. My brother's gay and he's in it.

Mavis says, It's no surprise American men are dying of heart attacks in record numbers. Listen to us talk to one another. We know all these big heart words like angioplasty and myocardial infarction. If you scraped the plaque and fat out of the heart of every man in America, you could fill Yankee Stadium with it.

But it isn't just that, Mavis says, it's the stress, too. Just about every man I know is popping an aspirin a day, hoping to keep that elephant from sitting on his chest. The pressure inside builds up, all the things this formerly great country now forces men to keep hidden from everyone else, it's a wonder we all don't explode inside our cars during rush hour and litter the freeway with pieces of our clogged-up hearts.

It ain't what you let out that gets to you, he says. It's what you have to keep inside.

Secrets.

One of them is that if you buy a man a few beers and sit down with him, put a tape recorder on the table, he'll tell you things he hasn't told his parents, his brother or sister, his lover, his best friends, the woman he's been married to for twenty or thirty years.

Mavis is like that. He's sixty-eight years old, been married forty-eight years, and I know more about him than his wife does. Every white guy has a friend like Mavis, someone who tells dirty jokes in mixed company because he thinks women like it, who calls Michael Jordan 'My Man Michael' when we're sitting in the nosebleed seats at Chicago Stadium but calls other black men 'nigger' when we're back out on the street, safely locked in the car. If I got mad at every white man I know who said something racist or sexist, I wouldn't have any white friends at all.

My black friend Ray, who's also in the book, says guys like Mavis don't bother him much. White guys like Mavis are like mosquitoes, he says. There are a lot of 'em out there, but you just learn to shoo 'em away. There are plenty of worse types in the world than Mavis, he says. Wasps out there. Bees, hawks, eagles, vultures. They come screaming down from out of the sun and sting you good, or carry you off somewhere and drop you, smiling all the while. That's the way the Man works. Mortgage agents, police, car salesmen, personnel directors, folks running for congress.

Ray comes to The Sports Bar too, every Thursday night after we play basketball at the Y. He's married for the third time, has two daughters in college from his first marriage, likes to talk to the tape recorder. He says white women look good, no doubt about it, but he prefers black. He says he'd lay all day on an ant hill slathered in honey if Whoopi Goldberg would come to him in the night with those purple lips. That Claire Huxtable, too, on *Cosby*. Jackie Joyner-Kersee. Sheila E. Mercy.

Ray says he gets even with men like Mavis. Works for a tax service part-time in the spring, for the extra money, and says those smiling white guys pay a little bit more tax than they should every year, on account of Dred Scott, Emmett Till, Medgar Evers, Brother Malcolm, MLK.

He has a another secret, too. He says when he plays ball, he needs one white guy on his team to pass the ball, play a little D. Four gunners is enough, he says, you need one near-sighted white guy who's afraid to shoot. Would even take an old fart like Mavis, it don't matter. Then after the game, when the brothers are shaking hands and rubbing flesh the way brothers do, the white guy stands there looking puzzled. Nothing like a sweaty white man looking puzzled to make my day, he says.

'Cept for you, he says. You and that little tape recorder. I'm fixing to tell you something good, he says. Something you won't believe.

Every man in America could make the same claim.

There are some secrets all men have in common. That won't come as a surprise to most people. For instance, most men I know cheat on their income taxes. The nickel and dime stuff usually comes on Schedule A, Lines 14–17, Gifts to Charity. We'll give a broken radio to Goodwill and take a two hundred fifty dollar deduction. We'll donate a 1956 set of Encyclopedia Americana to the Boys' Home, with volumes A-C, R-T, and

X-Z missing, and take a four hundred dollar deduction. Bigger savings come in unclaimed income, cash bonuses, things like that. Those with balls of stone claim depreciation on their homes as a business expense. You have to be willing to go eyeball to eyeball with the IRS if you take that one.

All of us have at least thought of being with someone other than our wives or lovers, and many of us have done it, many more than you would believe. That's not much of a secret, I guess. It's very depressing, when you think about it. As a group, we can't be trusted, and everybody seems to know that. In business, on the basketball court, among ourselves, that's okay. A lie is part of the language. Deception is part of the game. But with our families, our girlfriends, it's different. Ray says we live in two worlds and have to be two different people, and no one can do that very long or very well. He says you can't be successful in both places. Ray knows this from experience.

Ray says, You take a young guy, the only time he'll say the words 'I Love You' to a woman is just after he has erupted into some part of her body. Let a few minutes pass, though, and his mind is wandering trying to figure out where the hell he threw his underwear so he can get out of there. Why is that? Why are we breathing fire one minute, loving that woman with every atom in our souls, and twenty minutes later or however long it takes, we're dreaming of ways to get away from her?

I don't know, Ray, is what I tell him.

But look at this now, he says. What if that's our biological destiny? What if we can't help it? What if all of us have been formed this way from the genetic soup, you know—one part genius, one part lust, one part guilt, one part selfishness, one part brute strength, one part cruelty, one part just plain evil, and ninety-three parts confusion?

If you're a woman, you're thinking, Yeah, right. Let every fuck-up in history off the hook.

If you're a man, what are you thinking?

I'll tell you.

~

WADE: The first female genitalia I ever saw belonged to Margaret Trudeau. There was a picture of her in a magazine. She was at some dance club sitting in a mini-ski with her legs apart, and she wasn't wearing any underwear. God, she was so sexy. You couldn't really see much, just a narrow shadow and a little hair. I think I was twelve or thirteen at the time, waiting to take my guitar lesson in this music store where they had magazines in the waiting area. I tore that picture out of the magazine and took it home. I don't know how long it was before I found out that at the time Margaret Trudeau was the wife of the Prime Minister of Canada.

PHIL: A secret? That's easy. I really admire a guy who drives his wife and kids to church on Sunday morning in the cab of his pick-up truck. Especially if his wife is squeezed over next to him straddling the transmission hump and the kids are squeezed between the wife and the other door. I just like to see that. It couldn't happen with me, though. We don't go to church, for one thing. And my wife won't even set foot in my truck. She hates it. She wanted a station wagon. How can I haul shit in a station wagon? You tell me.

RICHARD: When my kids were ten or twelve I promised them a trip to Disneyworld. We bought this huge plastic piggy bank and wrote "Disneyworld or Bust" on the side of it with a magic marker, and for a year and a half, the whole family poured loose change and spare dollar bills into the pig, even a five or ten on occasions, to finance the trip. Jason, that's my oldest boy, would cut lawns on the weekends and put half the money he earned in the pig. Occasionally we had to empty the pig, and we opened an account at the bank. When we had nearly one thousand dollars, I took the money and used it for a down payment on a used Toyota Camry. I thought it was the best way to use the money. I told the wife that the engine was about to die in the Buick, but that wasn't true. The kids were upset for awhile, but they got over it.

CHRIS: I'm gay and I used to fantasize about having really bad sex with Liberace on top of a grand piano, surrounded by candelabra. [Laughter] No, seriously. Secrets? Besides the fact that no one at work knows I'm gay? I can't think of any off-hand. That BIG one takes up all my energy, believe me.

GARRETT: My partner in our law practice died of a heart attack right in the office—collapsed in the hallway and died. It was a shock. He was one of those guys who'd never been ill a day in his life. We'd been partners for thirty-four years, had gone to UVA law school together. He was like a brother to me. I know that's a cliché, but it's true. I was godfather to his son, and he was godfather to mine. His boy is in law school now, and when he gets out he'll join my practice. And I'll treat that boy like my own son.

When my friend died, his wife Carolyn left a few boxes at the office and asked if I would clean out his desk and files. The poor woman was really broken, was taking Valium just to sleep. She didn't want to have to take the picture of her and her kids off of his desk and drop it into a box, and I can't say that I blame her. So I did it. I emptied out all the drawers, cleaned out the files, everything. And I guess I was curious, because I looked through his things fairly carefully. And I found something in there nobody knew about—not me or anybody, not even Carolyn. How can I put this delicately? Well—there's no nice way to say it. My friend was blackmailing a judge. Three thousand a month. He had records of payments, deposition transcripts he'd transcribed himself, even tapes of telephone conversations. The most recent payment was locked in the drawer, three grand, in hundreds, in a thick white envelope. I couldn't believe it. Here was the closest friend I had in the world. I cried like a baby carrying him to his grave. He was more successful, seemed more happy, than most men ever dream of being. How could he get mixed up in something like that?

Well, I gathered up everything—the tapes, the transcripts, the money, everything—put it in a cardboard box, soaked it all in gasoline in the woods out back of my house, and burned it. No one ever saw it but me.

That judge was at the funeral, too. Shook my hand and stared me right in the eye when he told me what a loss it was.

~

Mavis lost his only son in Vietnam. It isn't something he likes to talk about. It slipped out one day. It happened before I got to know him, and not too many people know about it. At first, I wasn't sure why he keeps that private. He wants to go to the Vietnam Memorial, but he won't go, he says, because he's afraid his wife will embarrass him. But I can tell that's not the real reason.

He says, When my boy—Michael—had his first haircut, his mother saved several locks of his hair in an envelope, and put it in the bottom drawer of her cedar chest. Sometimes now when she's out grocery shopping or something, I'll be home watching football or whatever, and I'll take out that envelope and open it. Goddamn if that hair don't still smell like my little boy. I expect to see him come toddling around the corner, eighteen months old again.

When did he die? I ask.

Nineteen sixty-nine.

And then he stops talking.

~

AL: This is kind of weird. My wife's a beautiful woman, she used to be, anyway. I guess she still looks good to me but other guys probably wouldn't say she's so hot, you know. She's had five kids now, three boys and two girls, and now I guess she's about forty-three years old and she's put on some weight. She's got a fat little belly which is covered with all these stretch marks that look like these little tunnels where nightcrawlers might crawl through. It's all mostly loose skin, a little dry. The texture is warm and soft like velour or velvet or something. When we get into it I work my way down her tits to her belly, and I suck in mouthfuls of that loose skin and suck on it, rub it with my tongue, and it makes my dick as hard as a flashlight.

BARRY: This is really awful. You're going to die when you hear this. Once I found a guy's wallet with like seven hundred dollars in it, cash from his paycheck, and it had pictures of his kids in there, charge cards, driver's license, and all this other stuff. So I looked up his phone number, to tell him I found his wallet, to ask about a reward, you know? He said sure, I'll give you a hundred bucks, thanks for calling, where are you at I'll come and pick it up. I said I'd think about it. An hour later I called him back and said, Two Hundred. He said all right. I said, meet me at the entrance to Kmart at two o'clock. I'll be wearing a Chicago Cubs baseball cap (I don't even own one, man). I called him back the next day and said I changed my mind. He started cussing me out, said he cancelled the charge cards, called me a punk. I tormented the guy after that, kept calling him every day saying I was still thinking about giving him his money back. But he got real rude, so I was like, fuck him, man. I told him I put his kids' pictures up in a porno movie booth. His wedding picture, too. He finally changed his phone number. I ended up mailing him the wallet with everything in it, even all the money. I don't know why I did all that. I'm really not a bad person.

~

Ray says, Okay, here it is. My daughter Kayla has this friend, all right? Her name is Michelle. She's a junior in college like Kayla, from Mississippi or Alabama someplace. I see her here all the time. They're roommates but spend more time here in town than on campus. About two weeks ago they were over to the house. My wife was gone with my son, and it was just the three of us, watching T.V., listening to some music. They were going out to some nightclub dancing, so Kayla went upstairs to take a shower.

I'm looking at Michelle and she's looking at me, you know. We get to talking and we really get along. There's something happening here, see. I ask if she has a boyfriend and she says, no. I ask her if she has class on Thursday nights, and she says no. Well one thing leads to another and finally I end up asking her if she knows where the West YMCA is and the Super 8 motel next door. She says yes, and laughs. And that's it. Kayla comes down the stairs and they go. They hug me goodbye, first Kayla and then Michelle. Michelle says, eight o'clock at the eight? and laughs again.

Now I know what you're thinking, Ray says. I'm happily married and I fell into this trap before. But I'm smarter now. I learned my lesson. It's all harmless talk, playing around, that's all. Just talking.

It's just talk, I say.

That's right, he says.

On Thursday night, Ray doesn't show up for basketball. When I leave to go home, I see his car is in the lot.

~

CHARLIE: This is kind of a long story, but it's true I swear to God. One summer I worked third shift as a fueler at a truck stop on I-40 in Greensboro. It was between my sophomore and junior years at UNC, and I was living at home, saving money for tuition. Anyway, there was a third-shift waitress there who was also a prostitute who went by the name of Penny. The joke among the fuelers was to say, 'Her name's Penny 'cause she'll give Lincoln head.' I know it doesn't make sense, but it seemed clever when I was twenty.

This Penny could curse like a sailor going to hell but she was so beautiful—all this long hair falling all over the place, thin, sun-tanned, with these amazing green eyes. She lived in a trailer someplace with her brother, is what I heard. I got to know her pretty well. We used to get stoned together after work, just as the sun was coming up, and she used to tell me what it was like to crawl up into those rigs and do whatever those truckers wanted, within reason. She had a wage scale and everything, twenty-five bucks for this, fifty for that. She said one guy paid her ten bucks just to piss on his lap. That's the kind of pervs that passed through that place. Most of them were more normal, just wanted what Penny called the ol' number one (head) or number two (standard face-to-face sex, man on top). And Penny always used a condom, even before it was vogue. If you opened the hatchback of her Ford Escort, you'd see condom packets scattered all over the carpet like colored leaves.

One night this guy came in half drunk, cursed us out for not getting all the splattered bugs off his windshield the last time he was there—a fat guy with a huge belt buckle the shape of Texas and a Richard Petty cowboy hat with the feathers, you know. Chaw stains between his teeth. Last thing he said was to park it in the dark because he had a date with his girl. We knew that meant Penny, but we didn't worry much about it. She could take care of herself okay.

I didn't see Penny after that until it was almost light. She was sitting in a booth with Faye, one of the older waitresses, sitting on a towel full of ice. Mr. Texas had ripped her up pretty good, tied her up and did to her the only thing she didn't allow, and she was bleeding. She said she could look out his windshield and see us the whole time, but we couldn't hear her screaming because with all those diesels idling in the lot there's a constant rumble that makes your ears ring when you drive away from the place. The ice was helping a little bit, because she laughed when she saw me and said her asshole was frozen. Then she put her head down and cried. There wasn't anything she could do because everybody in the place knew what she was. Faye kept telling her to call the police, but she wouldn't.

Near the end of the summer, Mr. Texas came through again, this time all smiles and Mr. Apologetic. Said to Penny that he understood if she was mad, but slipped her a hundred and said no hard feelings. Penny took it, but ignored him. Custom was that for regulars, for three bucks, the waitresses would fill up their thermos bottles with strong coffee before they hit the road, and Penny did that for Mr. Texas just as he'd asked. He went out smiling, slapping the backs of the other Road Kings in the place, climbed up into his rig and roared off.

We found out later that Mr. Texas had driven his rig off a bridge in Kentucky and it had rolled some fifty yards down an embankment. Mr. Texas was killed in the wreck. I guess they found some of his teeth up near the top of the hill, so he bounced around in the cab pretty good. The coroner found enough cocaine in his system to kill a mule.

The waitresses all smiled at one another when they heard the news. I never told anyone about that, didn't even talk to Penny about it. Last I heard she ended up marrying one of the truck drivers and was living somewhere in Florida with six or seven kids.

HENRY: I'm eighty-four years old and I met my wife by accident, that's my secret. Got all spruced up one night, walked up to the door of what I thought was Judy Langley's house. Rang the doorbell. Door opened and there was Dorothy Parker. I had the wrong house. Now I'd seen Dorothy in school a few times. I thought she was pretty but honestly didn't think much of her. But there she was. I had flowers in my hand because I was going to ask Judy out on a date (this was in the Depression and we didn't have a telephone). Well, Dorothy's eyes just sparkled when she saw those flowers—which I had picked at the cemetery on the way— and I didn't have the heart to tell her they weren't for her. She invited me in for lemonade, which was sour because they didn't have sugar. Then we went for a walk and wouldn't you know it we fell in love right then. Dot—that's what I called her—always told everyone I came to the door as a stranger with flowers and swept her off her feet. I never had the heart to tell her it was all a mistake, that I was really coming to see Judy Langley, who lived next door.

STEVE: I was living with this girl, Susanna Raines, in a three-story apartment in Milwaukee, and we were thinking about getting married. We were both kind of afraid to go ahead with it, but sometimes we'd look at rings and laugh about it. Susanna even tried on some wedding dresses once. One night someone banging on our door woke us up and we heard people running outside in the hall. We could hear somebody screaming.

The building was on fire. When I opened the door all this smoke came pouring in, and I just freaked out. I said, it's a fire, and I just panicked and took off running down the hall. We were on the first floor and I just headed right out. About a minute later, Susanna came out, dressed, with a blanket around her shoulders and carrying another blanket for me. She handed it to me without saying a word, and we stood there on the sidewalk across the street watching our building burn, red lights flashing all around us. Susanna would look over at me and I could see she was crying. We broke up the next day.

I really missed her after that, too. So it wasn't that I didn't really love her because I did. I don't know. I panicked. I just ran out and left her in there. If the fire had been a bad one she could have burned to death.

~

Ray and I met playing in the men's over-forty league at the Y. He's a hell of a player for a guy his age, can still run the floor, hit the rhythm jumper off a pick. We were in the locker room dressing next to one another, and I mumbled something because I had forgotten my shirt. Ray had an extra and he tossed it to me. It was a black t-shirt, and across the front, in gold letters, it said, "Black by Popular Demand." I wanted to turn it inside out, but I didn't.

Everyone had a field day with that. I walked onto the court and every black guy in the place just busted up. Afterward, I told Ray I'd have it washed and I'd bring it back next time. He said that was fine, glad he could help. That's how Ray is. He's about the nicest guy I ever met. I said, let's grab a beer, and we did.

This Thursday, Ray isn't so chatty at first.

Missed you last week, I tell him, as we're lacing up our shoes.

Let's just play, he says.

Later, Ray talks. He says, Okay, so I went ahead and did it. Man, that girl is beautiful. I don't know if it's that southern accent or what.

You slept with her.

Yes I did, he says, and home by nine-thirty, like always.

I don't know Ray, I say.

He says, We're going to meet again Saturday. I told my wife I'm going to be at your place watching boxing on cable.

~

NATHAN: This is a story from my childhood and it's really ironic. When I was a kid, there was this boy with Down Syndrome in our neighborhood named Johnny Dreyfuss who used to ride around on a yellow five-speed bicycle wearing a ski mask. Johnny was a short, thick kid, probably about fifteen at the time. Kids called him a retard. He had these really strong legs from riding his bike all day long, and he could ride faster than any of us. We were all eleven or twelve, I think. Maybe a little younger. We would have these races down this long, steep gravel road that came into the subdivision, and Johnny could win easily. Sometimes we tricked him and said GO! and the rest of us would stay up there and laugh while he peddled madly for the bottom. So we weren't nice to him, I guess that's obvious.

That summer this new kid moved into the subdivision named Bennie Drath, a little fat kid with a brand new ten-speed bike. He whined and cried all the time and none of us liked him, and we were jealous of his bike, too.

One afternoon, we were all lined up on top of the hill for a race, and way down at the bottom we could see Bennie coming up the hill. We could hear his shrill little voice yelling, "Wait for me! Wait for me!" I looked at Johnny and told him to ride down the hill as fast as he could and run over Bennie. Johnny smiled and nodded about twenty times, like he did, and took off. Just like that. I was only half-serious when I said it, but before anyone could say anything Johnny was steaming down that hill, hunched forward over his handle bars, drawing a bead on little Bennie Drath and his new ten speed.

To Bennie's credit, he seemed to sense what was coming, and he turned and tried to get out of the way. But it was way too late. Johnny hit him broadside, going full speed, and we could hear the collision all the way up the hill. Bennie and Johnny ended up fifteen feet down the hill, tangled together in the spokes and bent frames and flattened tires of their bicycles. Bennie had a broken arm, scrapes all over his body, and a cut on his forehead that required seventeen stiches to close. Johnny had flown off his bike and skidded, and he was bloodied beyond belief. All the skin on the palms of his hands had peeled off in the gravel, and he kept touching his shirt leaving bloody palm prints, trying to stop the bleeding. One of his handlebars had gored him in the throat. Their crying alerted one of the neighbors, and she called their moms.

Johnny took the blame for everything. His parents didn't allow him on a bicycle the rest of the summer.

I say that's ironic, because it is. My wife Gail and I just had our second child, and she has Down Syndrome. So in a way, growing up with Johnny Dreyfuss in the neighborhood helped me, even though I did about the cruelest thing anybody ever did to him. If something like that happened to Lauren, I think it would kill me, I really do.

~

Mavis says, You have a son and you try to raise him right. You promise yourself you'll raise him like your father raised you, but without the mistakes, without the shouting and the temper. You want him to love his country, get a good education, marry a nice girl. Every night you fall asleep afraid that something will happen to him. Doesn't matter if he's two or twelve or seventeen.

Mavis looks at the tape recorder. Turn it off, he says.

What?

I don't want you to record this.

I shrug and turn the machine off, then back on. Wouldn't you do the same thing?

Is it off? Mavis asks.

I nod.

Mavis says, When Mike drew a high draft number, five I think it was, he just wandered around all day, looking lost and really scared. I didn't know what to say to him. We couldn't afford to put him in college, and I don't think he wanted to go to school, anyway. God, did my wife cry. Her little boy was going off to war.

When his draft notice came, my wife hid it from him. I had to pry it out of her hand. He told her not to worry. He hugged her. He said, Don't worry, Mom. I'm not going to Vietnam. Next week, me and a friend are driving to Canada. I didn't say anything.

Late that night, after his mother was asleep, Mike and I took a little drive. I blew up. I said no son of mine was going to run away from serving his country. I said if he went to Canada he better stay and change his name, because he couldn't use mine anymore. I said all kinds of things. I sounded like my father. Mike started crying. He said he was afraid. He said he was sorry, that he never meant to disappoint me. God, he was a hell of a kid.

Next morning, he told his mother he changed his mind, never brought me into it at all.

You carry something like that around your whole life. Rusts your insides out.

~

B.J.: The first time I saw *Bambi* I cried. I guess I was ten or eleven. I saw it again a couple weeks ago, and I had the urge to walk out. I would have, too, but I didn't want to leave my kids in the dark theater alone with all the perverts that are running around. They talk about MAN in that movie like he's some kind of fuckin' monster. Did you know that?

GEORGE: I secretly read my girlfriend's *Cosmo* to find out what the babes think we're thinking. There's some pretty crazy shit in there, believe me.

MAURY: You'll laugh at this. I'm a podiatrist with a foot fetish. [Laughter] Honest to God. When a woman with beautiful feet comes in, especially if she's wearing toenail polish, I get a hard-on so fast I have to excuse myself to button my lab coat. The woman can be as ugly as a battle horse, but if she's got nice feet, boing!, up goes the periscope. Sometimes I get about ten erections a day and when I get home I can barely make it through supper before I pull my wife into the bedroom. [More Laughter] You don't believe me, I can tell. She's a size seven, narrow feet with long, beautiful toes. I buy her sandals every year for her birthday.

GREG: I did a threesome with both of my ex-wives. They were good friends even before they had me in common, and it was their idea. It was pretty weird, man. I don't think I'd do it again. It wasn't really like sex. It was more like trying to juggle and tap dance at the same time.

~

Ray says now this Michelle is all he ever thinks about. She's a plague on my mind, he says. I can't concentrate. I can't even balance the fucking checkbook. Why does this always happen?

She's less than half your age, Ray, I tell him.

She's an adult, he says.

That's not the point.

Don't answer your phone this weekend, Ray says. Let your machine do it. Screen your calls. I told Anita you and I were going fishing, that we'd be back Sunday night.

Ray.

Thanks buddy.

~

ALBERTO: There's this girl at the bank, really a hot little number. I got my own little vending business, I go in every day, so I see her a lot, right? And she sees me. So one time I go in, and she counts out all the change, and then when she gives me my book back there's a note in there. It says, meet me at this place at noon. So I'm thinking, what the hell is this, you know? But of course I go. Who could resist that, right? She calls me over to her car. I get in. She hardly says a word, just drop your pants. So I figure what the hell, and I do. I mean my pecker's already springing to attention, so I figure she'll go down on me. She pulls off her necklace and drapes it over my dick. Then she pulls out this marker, this yellow highlighter like you used on Cliff's Notes in college, and she colors my pecker yellow. That's some funky shit, right? And that's it. That's all she does. She puts the cap on the marker and says, I have to get back to work. She took her necklace back and started the engine.

I think my pecker stayed yellow for a week.

HAROLD: I hate retirement. That's it. All while I was working, I was counting the days until I could retire. Some mornings, that alarm clock would go off, it was all I could do to drag my ass out of bed and go in. But now that it's here, it ain't what I expected. You find out that without your job to talk about, you're not a very interesting person. You find out life was easier when you weren't with your wife all day. People tell you, get a hobby. What am I gonna do, build ships in bottles or some crap like that?

NEIL: When I was a kid, my brother and me shoved a firecracker up the ass of our guinea pig. We had to finish him off with a shovel. There was blood all over the grass, so we told our parents a dog got him.

⌒

Thursday, Ray's back at the Y again, throwing elbows, running the floor, playing to win.

Later, he says, Michelle was unbelievable. I don't think she even put her clothes on the whole weekend, just went from the bed to the shower, back to the bed. That girl just soaked me up 'till I was dry. And then Sunday afternoon, I'm in bed watching the Bears on T.V., and she says she had a great time but she can't see me anymore. It's over. Sorry. Goodbye.

What?

She says she and my daughter are really close, and she doesn't want to jeopardize their friendship.

⌒

ANTHONY: I dated a white girl for a year in college and never told my parents. They're big into the NAACP and all that, and if they knew I was sleeping with Cinderella they would have flipped out. Her parents were pretty cool about it, though. I can't say I like white girls any better than black girls, though. I like all women in general. That's like a stereotype, right? A black guy who sleeps around with all kinds of women. It's bullshit. White boys do the nasty and run just as much as we do.

JEFF: I just had my second kid, my wife had it, you know what I mean. And I love those kids more than her, something I didn't expect. I mean, having kids turns you into someone else. Before, it was like, life is okay, let bygones be bygones, you know. But when you have kids, it's like, touch my kid and you're dead. I seen this bumper sticker on a guy's truck. It said, My Wife—Yes; My Dog—Maybe; My Gun—Never. For me it would be, My Kids—Never. I love 'em so much I have hate in me now. For the first time, I think. I told my dad about this and he's like, That's Responsibility, Son. And I'm like, right Dad, responsibility is what would make me burn a guy's eyeballs out with a blowtorch for looking at my little girl. I wasn't prepared for this.

⌒

Mavis shows me an airline ticket, says he's flying to the Wall this weekend, alone. His wife's sister is having gallbladder surgery, and his wife is going to Iowa for a few days to be with her.

So I bought the ticket to D.C., he says. Now or never. I'll be there and back and she'll never know I was gone. And then he shows me something else. He takes a piece of folded paper from his pocket. It's so old the creases are soft, almost worn through, and the paper itself is like cloth. Carefully, he opens it up. He hands it to me.

Mike's draft notice, he says. He pulls a cigarette lighter from his shirt pocket. It'll be a start, he says. We can burn it together, Mickey and I.

∿

And so the tape recorder runs, and I already know there isn't going to be a television series or a men's cologne named *American Apollos*. The book isn't shaping up to be, "a paean to the tenacity, courage, and soul of the American male," words my agent has already written for the book flap.

It's becoming something else. Something far less marketable.

But these are some of the men I know. If it will make you feel better, I admit that sometimes even I can't recognize them. As I listen and transcribe their voices, sometimes I can't believe what I'm hearing. Because I know these guys. They're good, decent, hardworking guys. Really. They'd do anything for you.

∿

MARVIN: If I had my life to live over again, I would do everything completely different. Like what? Like go to a different school. Wear my hair different. Marry a different girl. Take up a different career. Go to a different heart surgeon. Live somewhere else. Be someone else. Die satisfied.

MARVIN: [One minute later] I was just joking. [Laughter] Life is grand. Life's a fucking bowl of cherries.

Cyclone Eddie King

I WAS SITTING at the office last week trying to decide whether to bet the Lakers and take the points or whether to give the points and bet Detroit, and my editor calls me to his desk and says he wants a feature on Eddie King for next week's paper. You were there, he says. Call the coaches, the doctors, his girlfriends if you have to, but get to the bottom of that story. I'll give you a week, he says.

And don't spill any beer on it.

If I were any kind of man at all, I would have quit and told him to go to hell. To begin with, I'm not much of a sportswriter. It's a dead end job in a little high school town wilting in the shadow of Chicago, where all the blue chippers live. It's just a weekly paper called the *South Suburban Star*, with more grocery store ads than articles if you want to know the truth. But I go to the high school ballgames, the track meets, the catered awards banquets, and I type up boring little blurbs about how so-and-so placed fourth in the mile, and so-and-so scored fifteen points in the game, and so-and-so was voted most improved by his teammates. Get all the kids names in, my editor says. And spell them right for Chrissake. Don't need any angry mothers throwing curlers at me in the grocery store because you spelled Schichowski with a y.

But it could be worse. People know my name. I walk up in the bleachers, kids look at me. The men shake my hand. Women point and whis-

per. And every once in a while, I get to watch something special—a con-
ference championship, a state record. No goddamn Superbowl, I'll grant
you. But it gives you a good feeling, makes you happy to be alive in a way.
Then there's kids you see once in a lifetime—like Eddie King—with a
beauty you can't completely describe, the kind of kid who takes the body
to a new standard and drags the rest of us with him, like a Mozart in
music, or a young Bobby Fischer in chess. It's something mysterious and
magical. And when that magic fails, everyone wants an explanation. But
believe me, no one can tell this story.

You see, Cyclone Eddie King is like quicksilver on a wet rock. He's like
stocking feet on a polished wooden floor. I mean he's smooth as a cheer-
leader's thighs—got a little wink and piano key smile that could charm
the black dress right off a widow. Everybody who knows him knows it
too, which is what makes this story such trouble.

Used to be, Eddie was an extraordinary athlete. I'm talking Division
I, professional caliber. Had muscles that would make a racehorse cry—could
run like the goddamn wind, this kid. I saw him in junior high coming up,
a nice looking kid, a little cocky maybe. Already had hamstrings so thick
and shiny they looked like black earth turned over by a plow. Put a foot-
ball under his arm and it was like nothing you'd ever seen. In high
school, Eddie gained three hundred yards a game. Could run a hundred
yards in something like 9.2 seconds, and, get this: He could dunk a frick-
ing basketball with his little brother hanging on his back.

I saw that one myself. Drove by the playground one Sunday after-
noon and they're all out there shooting in the rain, no net, the rim all rusted,
paint peeling off the backboard. Eddie, he was a junior then, he starts
dunking—reversers, 360s, triple pumps, putting on a goddamn show,
and pretty soon he's got his little brother—must be seven or eight—up
on his back, arms wrapped around his throat, ankles locked across his
belly. Eddie, he starts out where the free throw line should be, bounces
the ball twice on the concrete and takes off (little brother holding on for
dear life, eyes bulging like ripe fruit). Up, up, up he goes, basketball
double-handed, cocked behind his head, his forearms shining like a
couple of eggplants, and slam! he tomahawks the ball through the rim.
Had no respect for gravity, this kid. And I thought then: Legs like that in
his mama's womb, the poor woman must still have bruises.

Eddie's high school career was glorious. I don't think I missed a game. Even the *Tribune* sent a guy out regularly to see the Cyclone. And Eddie, before it was through, he was the most famous kid in the neighborhood—folks had my news clips and photos taped to the glass doors of grocery stores, on the wall of the barber shop, even on the bulletin board of the dentist's office. Eddie's legs and my words, we were a good combination. But the best part of it was, this was just a kid playing for fun and doing things the rest of us could only dream about. I mean, one time I'm on the sidelines with a press pass looped around my neck, and Eddie goes flying by, loose turf spraying up behind his cleats, opposing tacklers trying to break his neck, and he winks at me and gives me a thumbs up. Effortless. The best picture I ever took—won some little award if you want to know the truth— shows Eddie leaping over a pile of tacklers at the five yard line, his knee pads clear over everyone's goddamn helmets, his thick arms covering the ball, and a wide smile stretched across his face.

His senior year, as you can well imagine, the kid's got college recruiters sleeping on his porch and climbing down his goddamn chimney. I mean, they're flying in like locusts from all over the country. Eddie says he wants to go south someplace where it's warm, keep his hamstrings soft and flexible. Chooses Alabama—wants to be a tidal wave in the Crimson Tide. Turns out, though, that his grades aren't too hot. One recruiter from California says to me, if Eddie's gradepoint average was an earthquake, it wouldn't even show up on the Richter Scale.

From there things only get worse. In the fall Eddie goes to some junior college in Missouri so he can pull his grades up high enough for big time ball. By then, already, he's fighting for his life. People are beginning to talk about how here was just another black kid who let it all slip away, who had the world by the ass but couldn't hold on.

The big news come in just before Christmas time: The Cyclone is dropped out of school. Rumors flying. One guy says Eddie opened a book and couldn't read a line. Another says he knocked up two coeds, rich white girls from out East someplace. Somebody else says crack cocaine.

But it was all racist nonsense, every bit of it. Eddie comes home Christmas Eve, plane lands at O'Hare in the snow, and when Eddie comes out of the tunnel he's wearing his blue high school letterjacket, and he's sitting like Buddha in a silver wheelchair. Paralyzed. I says to myself, Oh Lord, now what the hell you done?

~

As for me, I never had an ounce of ability athletic-wise. Bowl a few frames here and there, play some softball and a little poker, but that's about where it stops. Got a bit of a pot hanging over my belt buckle, smoke and drink too much, got an ex-wife who thinks her sole purpose in life is to keep my blood pressure in the danger zone. Spend at least half my time sitting on my ass in the dark. There's a group of regulars who hang out at Barney's Tap on Orchard Street, across from the high school, call ourselves the weight lifters. We must have lifted a hundred semi-trucks of Budweiser in our life, twelve ounces at a time. That's our claim to goddamn fame.

There's four of us most of the time, and it's the closest thing to family any of us has got. Barney—he owns the place and lives upstairs with his wife and about six dogs—calls us the four quarters, because he says sometimes it takes all four of us together to come up with a buck. After me there's Marvin Harris, who chews cigars and bets the Bears like a madman, and Johnny Drake, at thirty-seven the youngest of us, a garbage man. Kid pulls in a good buck, but he smells like rotten vegetables all the time and hasn't saved a penny in his life. Next is Hal Wisniewski, who became a born-again Christian after he found out he had diabetes and his legs were going cold. He's a drunk like the rest of us, but a holy drunk. He doesn't get along too good sometimes with Marvin, who will blaspheme the Mother of God if it will help the Bears beat the point spread.

Anyway, Christmas Day it's the four of us and Barney, about three o'clock, watching a college ballgame. Someone, Johnny, I believe, come in with a gallon of egg nog, and Hal's wearing a cross about as big as a goddamn dinner plate. But we're enjoying ourselves, getting by, feeling good. Then the door pops open, the sunshine cutting through, burning our eyes, ice-cold wind whistling, and in rolls Cyclone Eddie King. He's got a two-piece pool cue tucked under his arm, biceps bulging out of his coat like footballs, one of those skinny cigars between his teeth. The glare off the chrome spokes of his wheels spins across the ceiling like a mirror ball at a wedding dance.

When the door slams closed, I can see just the shadow of him roll slowly to the billiards table, the tip of his cigar glowing orange like a sunset. Barney reaches behind the bar and flicks on the house lights above the table, and the green felt glows—just like a ballfield, I'm thinking. Eddie racks up the balls, screws his stick together, and lines himself up behind the cue ball. He draws the stick back even and slow, blows out two lungs full of smoke, and crack! he lets it go. On the break, it sounds like the cue ball's been split by lightning, and there's balls scattered all over the table, a few in the pockets, a couple more bouncing across the cold tile floor.

Jesus Christ, says Marvin, it's like he hit them with a sledgehammer.

I toss some change on the bar and bring Eddie a cold one, set it on a small table beside him. He winks and smiles, says thanks, then turns back to his game. Plays all afternoon and into the evening, me just sitting there, watching, drinking one beer after another. I couldn't believe it. Here's a comet fallen from the sky, and he rolls into Barney's to drink with us river rocks. Christmas goddamn Day.

Around closing time, it gets too much for me. I say, Eddie, what was it, a linebacker cheap-shot you? Spear you in the back after the whistle?

He looks at me but doesn't answer. The irises of his eyes are black and as large as dimes.

I say, Then you were up in the fricking clouds with a basketball cocked behind your head, and when you come down from the stratosphere, a little white shooting guard from Indiana undercut you?

He looks down and takes his cue stick apart, rolling it in his hands so that the small muscles in his wrists twitch under his shiny skin.

Then Eddie, I say, what could it be? I mean, Jesus kid, you got a raw deal. You could goddamn fly.

He doesn't say anything, doesn't even nod or shake his head. And I don't notice it right away, but now he's got the cue ball in his right hand, and he's squeezing that ball so hard the veins on the back of his hand are bulging, thick as nightcrawlers. And it may be my imagination, but when he rolls the ball back across the table, it doesn't roll true but wobbles a bit, like an egg would. Then he looks down one leg, tracing the crease in his pants with his eyes all the way down to his ankle. He's wearing leather high tops, unlaced, the kind you can pump up with air, you know, and when he takes a breath, drawing the wind in through his nose, the muscles in his thighs seem to swell like they're filling with air. And then it looks like one foot twitches a bit, then the other. Eddie exhales and winks at me, then rolls toward the door.

I have a feeling then that I need to know something I don't want to find out.

~

Driving into the black neighborhoods was never something that bothered me much. People talk about gangs and drugs and all that shit, but I never see any of that. Sure, sometimes somebody will slap your car at a stoplight, hit you up for a cigarette, maybe ask for a buck or two, but what the hell. Small price to pay when you think of the shit they put up with every day. Put a black guy in my car and let him drive through one of the northern 'burbs at night, see how far he gets. Cops would be on his ass so fast you'd think he was Al Capone.

I been through Eddie's neighborhood so many times I could drive through with my eyes closed. Lots of kids know me there, see me parked at the curb by the playgrounds in the summer, watching the pick-up games, drinking beer. Eddie lives with his ma and brother in a small bungalow near the railroad tracks. It's a house with an open porch in front, clapboard siding, gray paint peeling everywhere. The porch steps are weathered and rotted, snow drifted across them, one small set of footprints punched through to the door. Two pairs of thin, parallel lines run down the snowy sidewalk along the side of the house, with footprints down the middle.

Eddie's ma smiles when she sees it's me at the door. The house is bright but sparsely furnished, with colorful afghans thrown over the chairs and couch. A wooden cross hangs on one white wall, surrounded by framed pictures of Eddie and his brother. A small television sits on a wheeled stand under one window, Eddie's little brother in a chair watching it, watching *Oprah*. The tile floor is a checkerboard design, gray and white. Eddie's wheelchair sits empty by the door.

Eddie's little brother sees me and says, You comin' to write about the Cyclone?

Hush child, his mama says. But I nod.

It's Jesus, the boy says. Jesus don't want him to run no more. Minister says so. Don't want him walkin' neither. No sir. Wants—

I hear a muffled slapping behind me, through an open doorway into the kitchen. It's a quiet noise, getting louder. Eddie's shadow comes first, then the head, those hands and shoulders, the wide, wide back, and those legs, wrapped in a blue blanket to the waist, sliding across the floor.

—Wants him crawling, little brother says, in a whisper.

Eddie sees me, pushes himself up on his hands and drags his legs behind him into the room. It takes him thirty seconds to move twelve feet. Then he rolls to his back and pushes himself up against the couch, keeping his elbows sunk into the cushion behind him. The blanket pinned around his legs is covered with dust and dirt.

I clean these floors, I do, his mama says. It don't seem to do no good. She looks at me, imploringly.

You have a beautiful home, I tell her, but I'm looking at Eddie's legs.

She says, Lookit what Jesus done to my boy.

Eddie stares up at me and shrugs, and right then I'm feeling everything go wrong. I can feel the spiral binding of my notebook in my shirt pocket pressing the pen against my chest, but it's as if my own arms are paralyzed. I can look a kid in the eye and ask, How's it feel to be conference champ? or, Is 51.2 your personal best in the four hundred meters? But I can't do this. What do I want to know? I'm thinking. What am I going to say? I thought I saw your legs move? Are you really paralyzed? Are you faking it? Who am I to do that? If I find out, I've got to carry it around, have to write it all down, and I'm not going to do that. My editor would run the story on a page backed by grocery coupons printed in red and green like sheets of play money, and people like me, who get winded climbing the goddamn stairs, would cut it up into dollar-sized pieces to save a few bucks on their grocery bill. What's that worth?

So I stand there, just staring at those legs wrapped in a blue cotton blanket.

Don't feel so bad, Eddie's mama says. You ain't alone. Everybody come by, want to know what happen. Natural thing. My heart's already broken, bleedin' into my chest, and they come by sayin' here Mrs. King, bleed some more. Tell us how you're feelin', havin' your Eddie crawl on the floor like a baby.

I'm sorry, I tell her.

Oh, I understand it, she says. If it happen on the field, people would leave us alone. They could watch it on the T.V. in slow motion. Doctors could explain it, then. Seem to me it's a miracle we walkin' at all, any of us. It's the bad news that make us start wonderin'.

So it wasn't an accident? This is what I'm thinking, but the woman reads my mind.

Nobody knows what it was, she says. Eddie just call me up one day cryin', sayin' Mama I can't walk no more. I told him, Baby, come on home.

～

Driving home, I stop for a six pack and pull over by Eddie's playground, which is empty and covered with snow. The dirty shred of a tattered net is hanging from one of the rusty hoops, and I can see Eddie's face in it. There's a word hiding somewhere in my head, and after two beers I finally find it. Psychosomatic. In a war, sometimes, a soldier will just stop walking—will become paralyzed—for no apparent reason. I learned this watching M*A*S*H on T.V. But why would Eddie stop running, I wonder, when it's the one thing he can do better than just about anybody else?

In the *Star*, we run just a little blurb on the Cyclone, a celebration of his high school accomplishments mostly, with a picture, and then a somber note on his paralysis without much explanation. We finish with the announcement that an anonymous donor in town has established a fund for Eddie's family at Lincoln Savings and Loan, and we run the address so people can contribute. I passed a mug at Barney's to get it started. Got seventeen dollars, ten of it from Barney's till.

～

In two or three weeks, Eddie becomes Houdini with a pool cue, starts to hustle a buck here and there from guys wanting to come in and see the Cyclone. Marvin thinks Eddie found some trouble with the wrong kind of people, drugs maybe, crack or something, and caught a bullet. Johnny says it could have been a freak accident, something he's embarrassed about, fell off his bed and landed on a beer bottle, something like that. You read about those things, you know. He says you have a spinal cord that runs like a piano wire from your brain down to the tip of your tailbone, and if you snip it, your legs just go dead. You push the key but there isn't any sound. Hal believes it's God's will.

Marvin says to me, What do you think, superfan?

I don't know, I say. I just don't know. All I know is when a racehorse loses his legs, they put him out of his misery.

The whole thing though, Marvin says, is that Eddie don't seem so miserable a lot of the time. The college insurance has picked up the slack. He's got a shiny new van with hand controls. He can park right at the front door at restaurants and shopping centers. Hell, even Barney lets him use the driveway when he comes here.

Then Johnny says, That's right. And you know he's wearing pretty fancy clothes, a leather jacket, gold chains. You don't see us wearing that kind of money.

What, I say. I'm angry now and they can feel it. What you think? You think he's goddamn faking it? Is that it? A black kid on food stamps buying steak when you're frying hamburger?

Easy, easy, says Marvin. No one said nothing about that. It's just that he ain't so bad off, you know, all things considered.

All things considered, I say, *you* should be in the goddamned wheelchair. All your legs are good for is hanging like ballast off a bar stool.

Christ, would you cool off, Johnny says. None of us are happy about this.

We all wanted to see him in the pros, Hal says.

Yeah, yeah, yeah, I say. I know. I know.

~

Soon springtime comes and the snow starts melting, and the kids start coming out. Across from my place there's a small park, and it's like the kids sprout from the asphalt when the snow's gone. Inside a tall fence there's a basketball court, cracked blacktop. Poles on each end with steel backboards, red rims, and no nets. Kids'll bring their own nets, sit or stand on tall shoulders to put them on, and take them down when they're through. They make a net last half the year that way. Soon as February sometimes they're out there in high-tops they got for Christmas, dribbling through the puddles, blowing on their hands, laughing, going three-on-three, five-on-five.

In March, I'm thinking maybe Eddie can get into one of those wheelchair leagues, you know, with Vietnam Vets and others like that. I tried it once, some benefit the newspaper got in on, for publicity. It isn't easy, I'll tell you that. I spun around in one place mostly, like a man with his boot nailed to the floor. These other guys, huge arms, hairy chests heaving under their jerseys, their legs shriveled and strapped together, they roll up and down the court so fast it's like the real thing. It would only take Eddie a few hours, and he'd be great at it. All he does is drink and shoot pool. No one asks for autographs anymore. Newspaper clippings up on the wall behind the pool table, including the headline where I gave him his nickname—"Cyclone Spins For Record 423 Yards"—are yellowed from all the smoke, and to tell the truth by now I don't like going in there too much. But I got nothing better to do.

Then one afternoon, a Sunday it was, week or two after Easter, we're all of us sitting along the rail, drinking beer, watching the NBA playoffs on television. Eddie, as usual, is at the billiards table in his wheelchair, practicing trick shots, shooting with his cue behind his neck, making three balls at once, things like that. There's a few guys watching him, sucking on celery that they're dipping into their Bloody Marys.

This strange guy comes in out of the sunshine, lets the door slam behind him and sits down at the end of the bar. Barney gives him a beer, and the fellow sips it a little bit, nervously, like it's his first one or something. But he's about forty I'd say, with a mustache, nice hair. He's wearing a blue suit that's a bit too big for him, but he's a nice looking guy really, just different, you see.

So, says Marvin, where you from?

When Eddie was a franchise player, strangers were constantly stopping in at Barney's to pump the locals for information, something that might give them a recruiting edge. They'd ask us questions—What does Eddie's mother do? Does she date anybody? Does Eddie have a girlfriend? Do they have family in such-and-such a state? We never told them much but always made sure to meet them, find out what university they were from.

This guy, he stands up, walks over to Marvin and extends his hand. When he speaks, he's got a little bit of a drawl. I come, he says, from the house of the Lord.

Hal, he perks up a little, thinks he can finally share his testimony with someone who'll listen. Marvin rolls his eyes at us and says, Came all that way, did you?

It's not an earthly place, my friend. It's the home of the spirit, a sanctuary for the soul.

Jesus Christ, says Marvin, a holy lunatic.

Are you born again? Hal asks. Hal's a little bit drunk, or he wouldn't be so bold.

Through Jesus we are all born again, the man says, and then he rattles off some long quotation from the Bible. I didn't have my pad with me, so I didn't get it down. But I could have. After a game, in the locker room, high school coaches go on and on, and I scribble it all down pretty much as they say it and get it in the paper. Sometimes they'll call me later to change something, or they'll ask me to make up something positive, a great learning experience for our ball club, we showed a lot of poise out there, something like that.

I didn't notice it right away, but this guy has a briefcase with him, and he lifts it onto the bar and fumbles with the latches. I've seen his kind before at O'Hare, selling religious books. Once I had one of those Hare Krishnas, bald as a beer mug, trying to sell me some crazy holy book with a paisley cover. Those Krishnas, they shake your hand and stare right through you. You're running to catch a plane, and they stop you and it's hypnotic in a way. I gave him five bucks and told him to keep the goddamn book, grow his hair back, and stop making his mother ashamed of him.

This guy can't get his briefcase open, but Hal shuffles over with his cane—his diabetes is bad by now—and helps him. He's got his pocketknife out, digging at one of the latches.

I've come to show you something that is literally one of its kind, the stranger says. It's all I have. It feeds me and clothes me and renews my soul.

There you go! Hal says, snapping the briefcase open.

The man raises the top and shuffles around inside with his hand. There are papers inside, and some loose dollar bills, but he pulls out this little glass or plastic case, looks like the kind you get when you buy a decent set of cards, and he cups it in his hands gently, like he's holding water.

This, he says, is an artifact of the miracle of ages.

He's got us curious, and I know that's the way these guys work. We're all of us leaning towards him, moving in that direction.

Marvin, who's sitting closest, says, It's a piece of Kirk Gibson's bat from the World Series. The one he homered with. Cost me fifty bucks.

But Hal, who's basically a shy guy, drops to his knees. It's like he's praying, and his chin is level with the seat of a bar stool.

The holy cross, he says. It's a piece of the cross.

And it's like he *feels* this power, this divine weight pressing him to his knees. And the man doesn't even have to say anything and Hal is reaching for his wallet. It's brown and cracked along the creases, and he opens it with his thumb and just pulls out several bills—could have been tens or twenties because he doesn't even look, but they're all singles as far as I can tell. He puts them on the bar. Marvin slides one across to Barney with his glass and says, Barney, give me a refill.

What is it? Johnny asks. What is it really?

Jesus, Marvin says, annoyed, it's a hunk of wood, a pencil shaving or something.

It is the cross, the man says. A branch of the tree where they hung our Lord.

This kind of talk makes Marvin uneasy, so he heads for the bathroom. Then Johnny looks closer, and I'm next to him. It's a little piece of wood, kind of gray and weathered, but you can't see the grain. It's only about an inch long and maybe a half-inch wide. All you can hear now is the television—the announcer's voice, sneakers squeaking on the floor, and crowd noise.

Then I feel this nudge at the back of my leg, and it's Eddie in his wheelchair, rolling in between me and Johnny to get a closer look. Moses parting the Red Sea. He's got his pool cue between his knees pointing straight up at the sky.

The man holds the case down lower so Eddie can get a look. Eddie looks at it and shrugs, and then looks around at the rest of us, as if he's waiting for us before he makes up his mind.

Where'd you get it? Johnny asks.

Jerusalem, the man says.

How? I ask. This is how these things go. Just by your questions, he's got you.

How's not important, he says. On earth, seeing is believing. But believing is truly seeing.

Is he still here, says Marvin, from out of the bathroom, yanking on his zipper and walking bowlegged. He turns to go back in but mumbles, The hell with it, and comes and sits back down. He brushes against the guy kind of rudely as he goes by, but this fellow doesn't know enough to be offended. He's just holding that little box like its the most fragile thing in the world, and we're watching him waiting for what comes next.

Then Marvin gets this idea. He says, Ever have that thing out of the box?

It's sealed, Hal says, from the floor. Airtight, to prevent decay, like in a museum.

No, my faithful friend, the guy says, it isn't air sealed. I would not prevent the needy and the faithful from having direct and sacred contact with this holy relic.

I'll give you a five spot to open it up, Marvin says. The man nudges his briefcase open a little wider with his elbow, and Marvin pulls a wadded five dollar bill from his pocket and tosses it inside.

Then ever so slowly, the man opens the case. And I swear, as it opens, I have to think about breathing. He holds it up to Marvin, and Marvin reaches in with his thick fingers, dirt under his nails, picks up this little sliver of wood, and holds it over his beer.

Does it float? Marvin asks.

Hal is beside himself, his head shaking, his face going red, but the stranger just smiles like someone who has seen hecklers before. When Marvin drops the wood into his beer, we all gasp in surprise, but then Hal starts yelling like a madman and tugging on Marvin's leg when Marvin lifts the glass to his lips and chugs it all down before slamming the empty mug on the bar.

You're all a bunch of lunatics, Marvin says, and when he smiles, he's got the wood between his front teeth. With one puff of his cheeks, he spits it out at Hal. And then—I saw it but I still can't believe it—uncoiled by reflexes you have to be born with, the sinewy, black hand of the Cyclone fires out and snatches that little sliver of wood right out of the air. Then he opens his palm, the pale, wrinkled skin unfolding, and he looks at this little piece of wood, stares at it closely, then hands it back up to the man, who returns it to the case and snaps it closed.

You see, the guy says, looking around at all of us, the Lord can protect his own. He slides his hand over the money Hal put on the bar and puts it in his briefcase. Then he looks at me, at Johnny, at Barney, and when he sees that no more money is on the way, he closes the case and snaps the latches. Hal, with the aid of his cane and a little help from Johnny, gets back to his feet.

Marvin laughs and shakes his head. That's quite a show, he says.

May the Lord bless you all, the man says, and then he kind of bows his head at all of us and heads for the door.

～

The rest of that day and into the night, it's all anyone can talk about. Crazy Marvin, pretending to swallow a piece of a fake cross—and paying five bucks for the privilege, Johnny adds. After Marvin buys him a beer, even Hal loosens up a bit and chuckles.

And then around closing time, this thing happens. It's one of those moments when everything that you know becomes less certain, when you read that the plane you missed because you overslept has crashed, killing all on board, or when you wake up at midnight and smell cigar smoke—the brand your father, long dead, used to smoke. Marvin turns to put on his coat, and he mutters, What in the living hell. . . . The rest of us look to see what he's cursing now, and he's looking over by the pool table, and when I see it, I can't stop swallowing, because my throat goes dry as sandpaper, and I'm thinking that somehow maybe I'm a part of this. What we see is Eddie King's wheelchair, sitting empty. The Cyclone is gone.

～

It's been over a week since that night, and that's pretty much where things stand. Hal has taken over Eddie's chair. Doctors are about to take one of his legs below the knee, but he's getting around better now than he has for years. Quit wearing his king-sized cross, too, all of a sudden. Marvin, he's starting to go the other way. Still bets and curses like a madman, but says he intends to drink ginger ale now on Sundays, says it couldn't hurt. Watching the ball games on T.V., we'll see something spectacular, and someone will say, the Cyclone could have done that. All of us, every time the door opens, we think it might be Eddie coming back. We can't get it off our minds.

Of course, everyone's thinking there's a plausible explanation for this: a coincidence, a medical fluke, a scam, anything but what we're thinking it might be, you see. My editor says, You were there, just write what you saw. Is the kid a fraud or not? He says, call around, ask some questions, you're a reporter for Chrissake. But then I get angry. I ask him, How is it that the only black kids we ever write about are the ones that can run like the wind?

You're wrong there, he says. Read the police beat. We write about the slower ones, too, the ones that get caught.

See, that's the kind of shit I'm talking about, I tell him.

Don't turn Democrat on me, he says. Just write the story.

So I say, I quit. But I don't say it loud enough because he doesn't hear me. He just sits there looking at me. And if I were a stronger man, if I could have envisioned any other life for myself, I would have repeated it, would have told him to stick his little newspaper up his ass until he shit headlines. But I didn't say anything else. Some people can change direction, and some people can't.

Just write what you can find out, he says. This ain't rocket science. Make a few calls. Come on. Where can a nineteen-year-old black kid disappear to? Take a week, he says. See what you can come up with.

The thing is, Eddie hasn't shown up anyplace. He hasn't been at Barney's, not anywhere in town, not back at college in Missouri. Nobody has seen him. And I've tried to find out the truth, but it doesn't seem to be out there and available. Doctors in Missouri won't talk about it, citing confidentiality, like they do. Eddie doesn't have a girlfriend. And his coaches in Missouri say they don't know what it was—that one day he was running with a football like he was born with it in his hands, and the next he wasn't even walking. But his legs were shriveling in that chair, and that's a fact. I did see that. Thighs looked like softball bats in the end.

Eddie's mama is sitting on the porch when I drive up to her place, smiling like a woman delivered. No, she says, she hasn't seen Eddie. But she expects to, someday. She says, When Eddie's running so fast his legs look like spinning fan blades, no one come and ask me, how's he do it? When he jumps up on the roof of the porch from the ground to fetch his brother's baseball, no one shouts, it's a miracle! So now he just gets up from a chair, and my phone be ringing and ringing all day. Natural thing. But if you got to ask? She shrugs. She says, The answer will pass right through your head without stickin'. Write that down.

So you see my problem. My editor wants a story, but I know what I have to tell him. It's either a story that's been told too often or a story that can't be told.

I'm just not sure which one it is.

Taxidermy and Infidelities

IN RESPONSE to a telegram sent four days before my father's fifth marriage, I met him for a March picnic at my mother's grave in the Catholic cemetery in Superior, Wisconsin. The invitation had been extended to my sisters as well, all of whom had quickly decided, in a criss cross of long distance calls from Birmingham (Kathy) to Wilkes-Barre (Mary Margaret) to Boulder (Hannah) to Chicago (me), that the old man had reached a new low and they weren't going. "I will not attend this pathetic exorcism of guilt," is how my sister Hannah put it. From Chicago, I had the shortest drive, and I had vacation to roll over from the previous year. But these were excuses I gave to my sisters. I would have gone even without them, and, of course, they knew it. I was a man, as Kathy put it. I could not be expected to do the proper thing.

Dad left Mother for good when I was three, so I never really knew him as a father. As a parting shot of semen—the Grand Finale, my sisters, who were then in their late teens, used to call me—I was really an outsider to the family history that fostered their hatred. But I was there for Mother's illness and death, caused at least in part by Dad's desertion, though I remember little of it. In high school, Hannah summed up Mother's perfect Catholic life in a three word poem—a short haiku she called it—entitled "Mother," published in the high school literary magazine:

Virginity
Fidelity
Death.

My sisters tell me the marriage broke up because there was another woman—actually, there were two other women, one underage, or so a rumor spread by Hannah had it. There were also two illegitimate children, one by each of these women, the first of whom, ironically, had been born with six toes on her left foot—as I was. Perhaps because the chances against this same genetic malformation occuring in consecutive children of the same father and different mothers are incalculable, it has always been for me a source of wonder and pride, and has served to bind me more closely to this first of what would ultimately total nearly a dozen step sisters. But rather than do half of the right thing and marry one of these women, as Hannah put it, Father ended up with a third, his divorce attorney's daughter, herself a divorcee and the first professional exotic dancer in Superior, Wisconsin, who performed with two pet boa contrictors on Friday and Saturday nights in the backroom of the bowling alley. He moved in with Bebe ("See Bebe and Her Boa Constrictors" said the sign at the Five-Star Lanes) within weeks of the final settlement, and she became pregnant with his child, another daughter it turned out, almost immediately. She continued to dance well into her eighth month of pregnancy, supporting herself and Father with the money she made, since he changed jobs more often than he changed wives, and went for long periods without having a job at all. Thereafter, Bebe was referred to as wife number two (or W2, as Hannah, fond of abbreviation, dubbed her), and became only one in a series of unusual wives Dad ended up with after Mom.

Throughout these unsavory proceedings, according to Hannah, Mother stood by strongly, tending to her children, attending PTA meetings, staring down gawkers in the grocery store, even as the infamous low-life to whom she had promised a lifetime of devotion publicly courted three of the wildest women in town. After Christmas, she contracted pneumonia, curable in those days (this was 1966), but was unable to regain her strength, and shortly after the new year, she died. With the ground in Superior frozen, Mom was put on ice and buried properly on March 21, the first day of spring. We planted daffodils on her grave, and Hannah read A. E. Houseman's poem, "To An Athlete Dying Young." My sisters tell me that Father attended the funeral service wearing sunglasses and a Five-Star Lanes bowling jacket.

Hannah, who was eighteen and going steady, promptly got married and moved her husband, Ray, into the house. Hannah and Ray raised me dutifully as their own son. My other sisters, Kathy and Mary Margaret, were fifteen and seventeen, respectively, and they mothered me and occasionally took me along on dates to give Ray and Hannah privacy. Thus, growing up, I saw nearly every popular movie that came out with one of my sisters and a steady stream of boyfriends. Kathy let me sit next to her, with her boyfriend on her other side, and often held my hand, while Mary Margaret bought me popcorn and seated me in the front row, where she could keep an eye on me while she and Lee Dickey, who became her steady, necked in the balcony. From then on, really, though he sent Christmas cards and called on birthdays, Dad was disowned and force-forgotten. The name Gilbert Jenkins never crossed the lips of Kathy, Mary Margaret, or Hannah Jenkins, and the memory of Katherine Jenkins was held in sacred trust.

Growing up with my sisters and Hannah's husband seemed normal enough. Hannah and Ray kept us all together for about four years, and they put off having children until I was nearly in my teens. Kathy and Mary Margaret each married and moved out. Hannah and Ray had a child of their own, then another. For my thirteenth birthday, Hannah gave me one of Ray's condoms folded into a birthday card. Hannah believed that promiscuity, like alcoholism, was hereditary, and she wanted me to be prepared for the testosterone fits which were certain to follow puberty. For nearly three years in high school, I had no use for Ray's condom, flattened neatly like a coiled-up spring in its foil pouch in my wallet, but it was still supple and antiseptic-smelling on junior prom night. The next morning, when I asked for another one, Hannah hugged me and said I was old enough to buy my own.

That was 1978.

My relationship with my sisters was forever changed one foggy morning in April, 1979 when I received a handwritten letter from Father, postmarked in Milwaukee. It was only a page long, and I felt pangs of sadness to discover how little he knew about us. Without the double helix of DNA that coiled in our chromosomes, binding us together (although the strength of those coils, as I would come to discover, is inestimable), he would have been a stranger. Near the end of the letter, he listed the names of his other children—the one with six toes, Carol Jenkins, and Kay Jenkins (in those days, children always took the father's last name, even in illegitimate cases); the three he had fathered with Bebe (W2), Elaine, Patricia, and Virginia Jenkins; and Eleanor Jenkins, whom he had produced with a third wife none of us had yet heard of (W3). By then, he had had ten children by five women, three of whom he had married. His letter closed with a final request. He was divorcing W3 to marry a taxidermist he recently met, a woman from Abilene, Texas. He wanted me to meet him at the courthouse in Milwaukee, Room 346G, to be his best man. If I didn't come, he joked, he would simply ask a deputy or a criminal awaiting arraignment to stand in.

When Hannah found out about the letter she was furious, and from the moment I decided to go, she treated me like my Father's son, rather than her brother. Suddenly, by accident of birth, as the only son, I had become a conspirator in my father's shameful, orgiastic life. To the horror of Hannah, Kathy, and Mary Margaret, I moved in with him and W4 after their wedding, a spontaneous act I was unable to resist as a boy of seventeen (what boy would not want to meet THAT man, at least for awhile?), and I lived with them for one unforgettable year before they moved to Texas.

Charlene (W4) was a Texan who wore armadillo-skin cowboy boots and carried her own business cards—"Charlene Henberry, Taxidermy, Armadillos a Specialty." She was menopausal ("glory of glories," said Hannah, "there'll be no more children"), had hair down to her knees, was forty-six years old, and married my father because, she said, he had wonderful hair, and he made love with the fury of a hurricane. She had a network of old high school friends, former lovers, and truck drivers scattered across the Southwest, a few in the Deep South, who kept an eye out for roadkills. Almost weekly she'd receive through the mail the once frozen (but now thawed), newspaper-wrapped corpse of an animal—oppossums, roadrunners, dozens of large rattlesnakes, armadillos, lizards, various birds. If it was a particularly fragile, or large, or valuable specimen, she would hop on a Greyhound and travel to pick it up herself. I cannot shake the memory of seeing her walk off the bus at the Milwaukee depot carrying a dead wolf, wrapped in foul-smelling burlap, under her arm. "Still fresh," she said to me. "Didn't even have ants on the eyeballs."

But she was a taxidermist of consumate skill, and she sold her mounts at flea markets and county fairs across the Midwest. The house smelled perpetually of fur and salt, and there were stuffed animals crouched on every end table and staring blankly or snarling fiercely from every available wall.

Her masterpiece was a magnificent ten point whitetailed buck, mounted forward from the back of the rib cage. Charlene and Dad had found it in the country, a road kill, one or two days "fresh." Dogs and other scavengers had already eaten the dark flesh of the hindquarters, and birds had picked out the eyeballs. But Charlene had to have it, and Father lifted the stiff, stinking corpse into the trunk, the bloodied portion hanging out, oozing onto the bumper and license plate. At home, Charlene cut off the damaged portions with a meat saw, then they loaded the whole thing—three-quarters of the largest deer I had ever seen—into the freezer, to kill the maggots and other worms that infected the flesh. This was the thrill of taxidermy for her: the bold reversal of decay, the artful reconstruction of the glorious beauty of life.

In the morning, Charlene worked her hair into a single, thick braid which fell down the center of her back and went to work. For several weeks, she worked almost exclusively on the whitetail, fleshing it out and boning it, scraping and drying the hide. But this was not to be a common shoulder mount, the likes of which are standard decoration behind bars and above every successful hunter's fireplace. Charlene mounted the full animal forward of the hindquarters. She gave it taut, powerful shoulder muscles and a thick neck. The forelegs were tucked gracefully against the body, bent at the elbows, the feet curled under. The ears were cupped back, behind the antlers, which curled like ivory and split into ten points, each as long as a steak knife. This was a whitetail deer frozen in the act of leaping over a fence or a windfall, with every muscle group firing in proper order. And one evening it simply appeared, fully mounted, on the living room wall, with large cracks chiseled into the sheetrock above and below it, so that the deer appeared to have leaped magically through the wall. It was a spooky, yet exhilarating, performance, and Father rewarded her with his highest compliment. "Woman," he said, "that thing just blinked. Goddamn if it just didn't blink!"

Charlene also did a thriving business mounting whole fish and animal heads for sportsmen, and she mounted as well the occasional family pet—primarily expensive exotic birds and an odd hamster or guinea pig. This was an exceptionally lucrative enterprise, and after the hunting season in November, the garage floor was wall to wall antlered deer heads staring up at the joists, gray and purple tongues hanging out stiffly.

At first, I believed what attracted Father to Charlene was merely her willful eccentricity. She seemed different—less openly sexual—than the other women he'd been with after Mother. Bebe (W2) was, after all, a professional exotic dancer, and W3, I learned, was a young painter and performance artist who combined her two interests by painting her nude body with oils and rolling around on canvases, while paying customers—university professors, hippies, and others with an eye for the kinky and absurd—watched. Her most valuable paintings were those she made while she was eight months pregnant, easily recognized by the zebra-like stripes on the canvas caused by her stretch marks. But Charlene (W4) did not seem to be interested in sex at all, at least that's what I believed initially. She dressed in the most manly clothes, chewed tobacco while she worked, and went for days without showering.

But early one evening I saw Father's car drive by without the lights on, and I could faintly recognize something tied to the top of the car. This wasn't at all unusual, since Dad and Charlene almost routinely went for drives into the country to search for possible mounts, but it was raining quite heavily. It was rare for them to expose a corpse to water, because this "loosened the hair" according to Charlene. About a quarter-mile past the house, the car did a U-turn and headed back, pulling into the drive without its lights on. The "corpse" on top was Father. He was laying nude on his back on a blanket, legs and arms spread and tied to the bumpers with yellow rope. His body was wet with rain, and he was laughing and singing "Home on the Range." After the car pulled into the garage, I could tell by the noise I heard afterward that Charlene had climbed on top of Father without untying him. Charlene howled like a wolf as she straddled my father, and in between fits of laughter the two of them made various animal sounds as they made love long into the night. In the morning, I helped Father pull the dents out of the roof of the Impala with a bathroom plunger.

Charlene taught me taxidermy in the year I lived with them, but I never was any good at it. Fish were the easiest to mount, though the skin was very thin and you had to handle it carefully. They were without the difficulties of legs or complex mouths (though the gills, like bloody strands of feathers tied together, were a challenge.) But it took the eye of an artist to make a dead fish swim in the air along the wall, and I did not have that ability. The only animal I ever attempted was a chipmunk, which I killed myself with an air rifle as it nibbled on an orange rind beside our garbage cans. I violated a cardinal rule of Charlene's ("we make life we don't take it") just in acquiring the mount, and when I was finished, the chipmunk looked like a small-scale dinosaur, and the eyes kept falling out, so I flushed it down the toilet.

After a year in Milwaukee, Charlene and Father moved to San Antonio, and I decided not to go with them. I was almost nineteen years old, had graduated from high school, and I didn't want to go to Texas. Two years later, when I married Ann, my ex-wife, I invited Dad and Charlene to the ceremony, but they didn't attend. They sent a gift, two horned frogs mounted, dressed like a bride and groom, dancing. Both had wide, human smiles on their faces. The accompanying card, in Charlene's hand, said, "Found these on the road, killed by dogs but not tasty so intact. Our blessings, and theirs, Charlene and Gilbert."

~

For awhile, all of us appeared to have transcended our chaotic family life to form stable married relationships. Hannah, who married first, lasted fourteen years. But when her marriage failed, the rest of ours followed suit. It was as if all of us were waiting for the first domino to fall. First Hannah ("clunk," as Hannah said), then Kathy and me ("clunk, clunk,"), and finally Mary Margaret ("kerplunk"). I had tried to be a model husband with my wife Ann, the mirror opposite of my father in every way, and our first year or so together was good, if vaguely unsatisfying and unspectacular. Eventually the relationship disintegrated further, and we both tried for a time, unsuccessfully, to ignore it.

"Mark," she said to me that memorable evening, as we sat playing Monopoly, sipping wine coolers, "you're really so conventional."

I had just purchased Boardwalk to monopolize Boardwalk and Park Place, and I had enough cash on hand to put hotels on each. Ann was on Marvin Gardens rounding the corner, and I expected her to land on me. I thought her comment was directed at my strategy.

"These are the most expensive properties on the board," I said. "I always try to buy them."

"Why don't you wear suspenders?" she asked, suddenly. "All the young men in my office wear suspenders."

"I like belts."

"And you like wing-tip shoes."

"Yup." I placed my hotels neatly on the properties, the red roofs shining in the lamplight.

"Mark, I think we should just get divorced."

I know there was much more discussion and then some shouting. She was an ultrasound technician, and I used to tell her that she believed shouting helped her penetrate people, to get at the softness inside. That always made her angry. She was a wonderful woman, really—smart, pretty, open-minded. It wasn't the belt or the wing-tip shoes, either. Not really. As individuals, we might have been interesting, exciting people. As a couple, we were dull. The decision to divorce was sealed that evening, as I fiddled with my hotels and looked at Ann's empty chair and her pewter game piece, a man on a horse, resting on Marvin Gardens.

~

At Christmas following Mary Margaret's messy divorce, the four of us— Hannah, Mary Margaret, Kathy, and me—met at Mary Margaret's house in Wilkes-Barre. Hannah and Kathy each had two children they needed to cart across the country, but Mary Margaret's husband—in spite of the time consumed by his countless affairs—had become a mogul in the paper business, and, as Kathy told me over the phone when the final papers came through, "she got the house, and it's a big mother." Mary

Margaret had swallowed a bottle of pills and almost died during the trial. Giving her the house was the least the court could do, in our view.

Over turkey dinner in a dining room with a cathedral ceiling and a chandelier, Kathy voiced their common complaint.

"My shrink said this is Gilbert's fault," she said. "I mean, how can I know what a successful marriage is if I've never seen one? My mother was Annette Funicello and my father was Henry the Eighth. He put notches on his bedpost and she washed and dried her mouse ears every morning. Is that healthy?"

"Mother was perfect," Hannah said. "She was a perfect mother."

"Perfect for who?" I asked. "Not for Dad, obviously."

"God, Mark!" Hannah said. "What a revolting thing to say."

"I wouldn't say she wasn't perfect," Kathy countered. "But is perfect normal? No, perfect's not normal."

"And then there's Gilbert," Mary Margaret said. Over the years, they had gradually allowed themselves to talk about Father, but they had stopped calling him "Dad." "He sent Mark stuffed frogs for a wedding present. That isn't even close to normal. That is a gray area just above lunacy."

"We didn't get any doubles," I said, and smiled.

"You can joke about it," Kathy said. "You're not as screwed up as the rest of us because you didn't grow up with him like we did."

"Are we screwed up?" Hannah asked. "Speak for yourselves. I don't feel screwed up."

"No? Miss sleep only with men younger than twenty-five? Miss I-get-Christmas-cards-from-my-plastic-surgeon," Kathy said.

"Wanting to look young and liking fantastic sex is not screwed up," Hannah said. "It's healthy."

"And leaving a perfectly good husband for the boy who pumps your gas is healthy," Mary Margaret said.

"That 'boy' was twenty-two," Hannah countered, "and until you've been with a man who could make you pass out with pleasure I don't feel you're qualified to judge me."

"I wouldn't call having sex until you're unconscious pleasurable or healthy," Kathy said.

"Please!" Mary Margaret interrupted. "Children are present here."

"Thank you," Hannah said. She looked at me. "What about you, Mark?"

"What about me what?"

"How would you rate your relationships?"

"I'm here alone, aren't I?"

"He's his son," Mary Margaret said. "He's even more screwed up than we are. He even lived with him and one of his bimbos."

"Charlene," I said.

"W4," said Hannah.

"She's a bizarre woman, isn't she?" Mary Margaret said. "Stuffing animals and all."

"She was good at it," I said. "She wasn't a bimbo."

"But it's hardly something to aspire to, is it?" Mary Margaret said. "You could be a veterinarian or something if you want to work with animals."

"Maybe she just likes dead things," said Kathy, waving her fork, "dead things with flies and maggots all over them."

"This is a delicious conversation," Hannah said. "Can we change the subject?"

"Maggots look like rice!" said Kathy's nine year-old son, Jeffrey, somewhat triumphantly.

Kathy pointed her fork at him, and he looked down at his plate. "It trickles down," she said. "My shrink says so. Even to him," she nodded at Jeffrey. "Gilbert's fault, all of it."

"The reason we're sitting here without husbands or wives is we had no healthy model," Mary Margaret said.

"Marriage is learned behavior," Kathy added. "My shrink says that, too."

"That means it isn't natural," Hannah said.

"Not necessarily," Mary Margaret said. "Going to the bathroom is natural, but you have to learn how to do it."

"You sure talk about your shrink a lot," Hannah said to Kathy. "Are you sleeping with him?"

"Oh, please!" Mary Margaret said. "It sounds like a brothel in here."

"To answer your question," Kathy said, "yes, I do. But only at my option. And I don't pay for those sessions. I'm in control of my sexual life, thank you, unlike former days when I was married to the missing link."

"Oh, Steve wasn't so bad," Hannah said.

"Not if you're an orangutan," said Kathy. "Truth be told, it was like sleeping with Bigfoot."

"Ray didn't have any hair on his chest at all," Hannah said. "And then he went bald. In the summer when it was hot, he slept naked on top of the covers, and I swear he glowed in the dark. It was like making love to a bowling pin."

"What was Oliver like in bed, Mary?" Kathy asked.

"I'm not talking about Oliver right now," Mary Margaret said, and left the table. Hannah glared at Kathy, who shrugged her shoulders and said, "Sorry."

"Men are such jerks," Hannah said. "Present company excepted," she added, looking at me.

～

We continued to get together every Christmas, through the remainder of the roaring 1980s. None of us remarried. Hannah's and Kathy's children left home and got married. We all lost track of Gilbert, and might never have seen him again, were it not for the initiative of one of our stepsisters.

One day I was at the office and my secretary paged and told me I had a call from my sister. This was not all that unusual since all three sisters bought their insurance from me and abused our WATS number regularly. But the voice I heard on the other end of the line was not Kathy's or Mary Margaret's or Hannah's.

"Is this Mark Jenkins?" the woman asked.

"Yes."

"You probably don't remember me, in fact you couldn't remember me because you never met me." She sounded just like Kathy, but she talked faster.

"Who are you?"

"Carol Jenkins," she said. "I'm your step sister."

The following afternoon, we met for lunch. Carol was a tall, beautiful woman, the kind that caught your eye. She arrived wearing open-toed shoes, and all through the meal I casually tried to see her left foot to confirm she was who she said she was. This wasn't exactly necessary, however. Her voice and gestures were exactly like Kathy's, and several times I caught myself referring to information Kathy and I had in common.

"Did you drop something?" she asked. "You keep looking under the table."

"No," I said. "I'm sorry."

"Are you sure?"

"Well," I said boldly, "can I see your left foot?"

"Ah," she said, smiling. "You know about that." I heard her shoe drop under the table, and she swung her heel up along the table and let it rest on my knee. Her toenails were painted red, and there were only five of them. "The scar's just to the left of the third toe," she said. "You can barely see it through the pantyhose."

"You had it removed?"

She smiled. "My mother did. When I was five. I really couldn't wear shoes, since the extra toe was on top."

"Maybe I should have that done, so I can stop wearing double E shoes."

Carol dropped her foot off the table. "You have it too?" she asked.

I took off my shoe and pulled off my sock, then raised my leg and rested my calf along the edge of the table. "Mine's on the side," I said, "like a twin to my little toe."

She rubbed a finger against it. "It's really calloused," she said. "But you have very nice feet."

"Thank you." I put my sock and shoe back on.

"Gilbert really left us a legacy, didn't he?" she said. "Scattering his maker's image throughout the land."

"What's that?"

"That's Dryden," she said, " 'Absolom and Achitophel,' an English poem. I've met several of our other step siblings. I've got everyone's address, actually. I tracked them all down. It took awhile, believe me."

"What for?"

"I'm a psychology professor," she said. "I'm thinking of doing a book on serial marriage, about people who divorce and remarry over and over."

"Well, you've got the right father for it," I said.

"I suppose," she said. "But comparatively, Gilbert is small potatoes. He's—we are—the introduction, a personal angle. Four marriages and what, twelve or thirteen children. A decent life of debauchery, but hardly a blip on the scale when you compare it to the heavyweights. I've got notes on men in monogamous cultures who have married twenty-two times, fathered seventy children. Another guy, a truck driver, had seven wives at the same time in seven different states, with two children apiece. All seven boys were named after him, and all seven girls were named for his mother. And then for variety if you throw in mention of some polygamous cultures, in Africa, for instance, where some chieftain had over one hundred wives and three hundred children—I think I've got a book that will get me on the talk shows."

"Why do they do it?" I asked.

"If I knew that, I'd be rich and famous."

"Were you ever married?"

"Divorced twice," she said. "I've given it up."

~

When I called to tell Mary Margaret about meeting Carol, she already knew all about her.

"She's called all of us," Mary Margaret said. "She's kind of weird isn't she, writing a book about sex maniacs? Hannah and Kathy wouldn't talk to her, since Gilbert was in it. She asked me a few questions, things I could remember about Gilbert, if he ever came on to me, things like that. I told her, 'Don't be stupid. He's an asshole but he's not a pervert.' And that was that. It's creepy to think we've got all these step sisters floating around. Just think if we all got together for one big family picture. The photographer would have to stand so far back to get everybody in, you wouldn't be able to recognize the faces."

Through our step sister Carol, Father learned our addresses, and in a note appended to the invitation to his fifth wedding, he invited each of us—myself, Hannah, Kathy, and Mary Margaret, to our mother's grave for a reunion of sorts.

And so this is how it came to be that at two o'clock on a cold March afternoon, the anniversary of my mother's burial, I drive slowly through the gates of the Catholic cemetery in Superior, the snow squeaking beneath the treads of the car tires, the blinding sun warming the dashboard. I had tried, through conscious, directed effort, to live a life as close to the opposite of my father's as my will would allow, and in a single afternoon, that life would be lost to me forever. It was also to be one of those rare moments when anxiety and anticipation are not disappointed, when the event itself—whether it is a birth, a death, or a sexual encounter—overwhelms its preconceptions. Hannah was right—it was to be an exorcism. But it would be mine.

I parked below the hill where my mother had been buried thirty-three years before. I pulled in behind a pick-up truck with Texas plates. There were three lawn chairs in back, price tags still on them. I followed in my father's footsteps where he had punched holes in the crusty, knee-deep snow with his boots, between the rows of markers. The temperature was below freezing, but the sun was warm, and the short, early afternoon shadows cast by the gravestones looked blue against the snow. Near the crest of the hill, I could see tendrils of smoke rising above the trees. Father was seated in a lawn chair on my mother's grave, facing the headstone, warming his hands over a small fire smoldering over her heart. He looked very old, his face a map of sunspots and wrinkles, but he still had what people call a spark in his eye. A second lawn chair rested in the snow at his right. There was a picnic basket on it and a six-pack of beer. He waved at me when I approached, then reached over and took the picnic basket and the beer and put them in the snow.

"Here, sit down," he said, wiggling the arm of the chair. "You look good. Put on a little weight, lost a little hair. You look a little like my father."

"Christ," I said angrily. "You're sitting on her."

"What?" he said, looking down over each side of his chair. "Oh, it's all right. The ground is frozen, and it's a sturdy casket. Really," he said, responding to my stares with his usual jocular manner, "go ahead and sit down there. Go ahead."

I lifted the chair out of the snow and set it back off of the grave. Then I sat down.

"Aren't you a squeamish one," he said. "Must have got that from your mother."

"Obviously respect for the dead comes from her side of the family, too," I said.

"I suppose you don't like the fire either. Would rather I sat here freezing, waiting for you."

"Why am I here?"

He pulled a can of beer off the six pack and tossed it on my lap. "Here," he said. Then he opened one for himself. I remembered the chairs in the back of his truck.

"No one else is coming, Gilbert," I said.

He nodded. "Figured not."

We sat quietly for awhile, drinking beer, looking around at the cemetery. There were a few tall pine trees across the valley, and a breeze we couldn't feel on the ground caused the highest branches to wave softly. Behind us, a hedge ran the length of the grounds.

"Haven't been here since the funeral," he said. "It's all changed. Trees are bigger, the lands all moved around. More hills. People like hills in cemeteries. Like to think their loved ones are at rest with a view." He sighed and jerked a thumb at the ground beneath my chair. "Plot over there is mine," he said. "Side by side. Your mother's gonna give me hell all through eternity."

"Are you dying?" This was a theory Kathy had. "Gilbert has a brain tumor," she said.

"Not that I know of," he said. "Will someday, if that makes you feel any better."

I surprised myself. "The sooner the better," I said.

He chuckled, but didn't answer. He finished his beer, then opened the picnic basket and pulled out sandwiches, a bag of potato chips, and a stalk of celery, still wrapped in cellophane with the price on it. He held the celery up at me, but I shook my head, and he put it back in the basket. I took one of the sandwiches. He tore open the chips and set the bag down in the snow beside us.

"So how are the girls?" he asked. I didn't answer immediately. My sisters demanded that I not reveal anything about them, and I promised I would not.

"They're fine," I said.

"Yeah? Good. That's good." He took a bite of his sandwich and looked at me. "I have any grandchildren?"

I looked away.

"Probably do," he said. "From those three good-looking girls, probably have six, eight, maybe ten even."

"Four," I said. The number burst through my lips, like the spasm of an involuntary muscle. "From Kathy and Hannah, four." I said it with a vengeance, to disappoint his high expectations. But it had the opposite effect. He was thrilled.

"Four?" he said, smiling. "Four." He held up four fingers, as if to reassure himself, then he opened another beer.

"I'm getting married again," he said, "day after tomorrow."

"I know."

"That's right, you do," he said. "I got a best man already. It's her brother. Hope you're not offended. I didn't think you'd come. It would have been you, you know. You're my son. But she picked him. Big guy, too. Size fourteen shoe."

"What happened to Charlene?"

"Oh," he waved his hand and chuckled. "I really do love her, but it's not the same. Grinds all her food up in a blender. The woman's only sixty-two years old, and she won't wear her teeth."

"So you're divorcing her?"

"It's a no fault kind of thing," he said. "They're so nice about it these days. Bing, boom, fill out some papers, pay a little money, wait a few months. I just couldn't take it anymore. You know how it was. Just got tired of having all those animals staring at me with their glass eyes all the time. Looked like Noah's Ark in the full bath, what she called her 'pairs' room.' Sit down on the john and there's a pair of iguanas staring me in the face. Got to be so I couldn't tell what was living from what was dead. And Charlene was getting a little bit crazy about it, started advertising in the paper for animal corpses and wearing a beeper, so people could call her at any hour. We'd be walking at a shopping mall and her beeper would go off, people'd think she was a doctor, the way she rushed for the closest phone."

I laughed and shook my head.

"See," he said, "you think it's a little crazy, too." He took a long drink of beer. "My new wife's name is Barbara," he said. "Barbara Martin. We met in Austin on a rattlesnake round-up, of all things. Here," he said, bending over, "take a look at this."

He rolled up his pants leg and turned down his sock. He turned his calf toward me. A blue tattoo ran the length of his calf. It was a list of names—our names, children and step children, one atop the other—with my name on top.

"Put you on top 'cause you're the only son."

"She does tattoos?"

"Half right," he said, turning his pants back down. "She's co-owner, with her brothers, of Martin Brothers Funeral Homes. Owns three of them. She's a mortician, and for a few extra dollars, she tattoos the dead." He pulled his sock up.

I didn't know what to say.

"Really," he said. "It's a whole new thing. Husbands have little roses tattooed on their wive's bottoms, or their names tattooed on their breasts. Wives put their names on their husband's arms, inside of hearts, that sort of thing. Of course, you can't see it when they're laying there, sleeping the big sleep. But it's been good for business. And it's great publicity. There's talk she might get on Geraldo."

"Why are you doing this?" I asked.

"What?"

"Marrying this woman?"

"You don't approve."

"I can't even imagine what's in your head. It's like you live in another world. What you do to people, what you've done."

"I only have one life," he said. "I should spend it pleasing you?" He waved off my response. "Men are rewarded with kind smiles and nods for repressing what makes them feel most alive. Good fathers stay home and cut their lawns, change the oil in their cars, take the kids to the zoo. I know this."

"You killed mom when you left her."

"Is that what your sisters told you? She had pneumonia."

"I don't just mean it figuratively. If you hadn't left, she would have lived. So you really did kill her. She suffered, too. We all did."

"I know you did. I live with that."

"And all the others? You've left quite a wake, you know."

"I am just trying to live a full life. It's the only one I've got, as far as I know."

I wanted to punch him.

"When I was twenty-three, right after Kathy was born, I got sick. Ball cancer, if you want to know the truth. Told the girls Daddy was on a trip, and had one ball removed. Doctors wouldn't say if my chances were good or bad. I might have died right then, and you wouldn't be here. The girls would have cried over me, kept flowers here. I would have been eulogized as a family man, a selfless provider, taken in the prime of life. But in here," he tapped his chest, "I always had run-around in my heart. I waited, though. I suffered, too, through all of that middle-class, settled-down crap, insurance bills, taxes, endless jobs, car repairs. And oh, the boredom! All those Sunday nights watching *Lassie* and *Bonanza*. I was losing my mind. Finally, I just couldn't fit in the shell anymore. I just exploded. And what came out wasn't anger, or ambition, or evil. It was passion for *life*, plain and simple. I had enough juice left in one ball to make a baseball team, which I have done."

"With subs and umpires," I added, sarcastically.

"Well," he said, chuckling, "I might have gotten a little carried away. But Barbara, I believe she'll be the last one. I could be wrong, but I believe I'm too tired. She's thirty-seven, so I'll probably die of exhaustion, which is a good way to go. The best way. I carry no life insurance, so it's convenient to marry a mortician. Charlene would have stuffed me, and done a beautiful job of it no doubt, but with Barbara I can get a tattoo, too. Maybe a list of wives down the other leg. But you're the only son." He smiled. "Isn't that odd? I used to think it must have been the sickness, that my son juice was in the ball they cut off, and daughter juice was all I had left. But of course that's wrong, because you came after."

"Maybe someone figured to cut the tree off at one branch," I said. "That you satisfied the urges of a dozen sons, and no more were needed."

"Just a shake of the dice," he said, shrugging. "Might have been that, too."

"You know you damaged all of us," I said, not in a hateful way. "None of us have led a normal life."

"You mean I didn't play ball with you?"

"I mean you made it impossible for us to be happy."

"Happy?" he said, in an astonished tone. "What's 'happy?' You think your mother was happy? She couldn't talk herself into it, and it's what she would have settled for. She had beautiful children, a house with aluminum siding, everything she was supposed to want, but she didn't feel how she was supposed to feel. Don't let anyone tell you different. Happy is what a dog is when it's eating. Happy is when the price of gas goes down. Happy isn't anything."

"We're all divorced," I said. "And it was terrible for every one of us. Mary Margaret almost didn't survive. She took pills, and if they hadn't pumped her out she would have died."

He sat silent for a moment. At first, he appeared stunned. Then he smiled.

"What was she like afterward?"

"What do you mean?"

"What is she like now, for instance?"

"She lives in a big house in Pennsylvania. I don't know what you mean."

"I'll bet she's not bored like she once was. I'll bet she doesn't sit home Friday nights flicking through all those stupid cable T.V. shows. I'll bet she doesn't watch *Wheel of Fortune* every night after the news, watching Vanna spin letters while the cells in her body slowly die."

"I don't know what she does."

"Ask her. You just ask her."

"I will."

"And what about you? Does the wind of life still blow through you? Or have you snuffed it out?"

I stared across the valley at the tops of the pines swaying slowly in the imperceptible breeze. I didn't know.

"So there you have it," he said, slapping his knees.

"You're a terrible father, Gilbert."

"Yes I am," he said.

"We all hate you."

"Hate?" he said, and chuckled. "Hate will keep you going."

~

We all hate you. . . . Those were the last words I remember saying to my father, though I'm sure I said other, empty things before I left. I didn't go to his wedding in Austin, had no intentions to, really. After leaving the cemetery, I drove straight home to Chicago, a ten-hour drive, arriving home just before three a.m. I never told Hannah, Kathy, and Mary Margaret that I had betrayed them, that Gilbert knew of their children and their divorces. It would have sent them into an uncontrollable rage to hear that Gilbert thought their failed marriages were like ballast jettisoned from the sinking balloon of middle-class life.

I did call Mary Margaret early one Friday evening. I asked her what she was doing. She said she couldn't talk now, a young man was taking her to see a nude performance of Shakespeare's "A Midsummer Night's Dream" in Philadelphia. "And after that," she said, "we're having a midnight picnic in the Poconos. He thinks he's a vampire."

"Be careful."

"Don't worry, Mark," she said, laughing. "I'm not going to marry the guy."

~

A few weeks after Gilbert's fifth wedding, my short relationship with an airline stewardess ended bitterly when she accused me of lying about my sexual history because there were only two names on my sexual partners' list (what Hannah calls an SPL)—Rebecca Morgan, my date at junior prom; and my ex-wife, Ann. Exchanging the lists was her idea—the only wise thing to do in this day and age, she said. Her list, printed on computer paper, ran down the left margin nearly to the end, with the addresses and phone numbers printed on the right.

But now I am seeing someone new, a woman named Inez, who advertises in the yellow pages as Madame Z. I met her in the checkout line at Kmart, where she was buying seventeen bottles of fingernail polish. She is a palm reader and psychic, and she has told me that me that my sixth toe is like an extra root, holding me firmly to my destiny, and that it signifies untapped sexual desires. This is all crazy, of course. But as we sit naked in the darkness of her round bedroom, with the constellations of stars painted on her black ceiling, candles blazing on the nightstand, and she traces the lines in my palm with her long, index fingernail (painted black, with silver glitter glued on), I feel a hint of something I'd been missing—absurdity, curiosity, wonder, the wind of life?—and I remember Gilbert, sitting in the snow, talking about cracking out of the suffocating warmth of his shell. And even as I am writhing between the freckled thighs of Madame Z, and she is screaming and calling out my name and the names I went by in previous lives, my eyes are closed, and what I see is Gilbert, mounted in his lawn chair, his glass eyes twinkling, a smile permanently hardened on his face.

Crickets

AT FIRST, Robert and Sara joked about it, called the boy their little entomologist.

"Look!" the boy would say, a dirty fist thrust toward them. His hand would bloom and a cricket would appear, a dark stamen in the flesh of his palm.

"How many is that, now, Alex?" Robert would ask, as the number climbed. Eleven. Seventeen. Thirty-one. Sixty.

"Sixty!" His parents laughed together at the new number. Sixty crickets. Thirty in each red Hills Brothers can on his dresser, thumping off the plastic lids like popcorn.

"Where does he find them all?" Sara said.

"Maybe he'll be a famous entomologist someday," Robert said. "The Einstein of bugs."

"Or else he'll be the Orkin man," said Sara. "One or the other."

One night, as Robert and Sara read the evening paper, Alex sat down on the floor with two library books, *The Wonderful World of Insects* and *A Field Guide to Insects and Spiders*.

Alex read aloud. "In sixteenth-century England, kings and queens kept song crickets in gilded cages of silver or gold."

"Is that right?" Robert said.

"In many parts of the world," Alex said, "people eat crickets. A cricket contains as much protein as six ounces of beef."

"Imagine that!" said Sara.

"In parts of China and Japan, crickets are kept in elaborate cages made of steamed bamboo, or carved from ivory. Some poor Chinese grow gourds inside of glass bottles to shape them for cricket houses. Cricket fighting is also a popular sport in China. To strengthen their crickets before a fight, trainers will feed them mosquitoes engorged with blood from their own arms. To anger crickets for battle, trainers will tickle their soft undersides with brushes made from coarse rat hair. Winners are esteemed and bred to produce strong offspring. The losers are fed to goldfish."

Alex looked up at them.

"Mom," he asked, "do we have any more coffee cans?"

The following day, Robert took him to Kmart, where they purchased a thirty-gallon aquarium and wire screen for a cover. On the floor in the boy's room, the bottom a mat of field grass, the aquarium soon swarmed with over one hundred crickets.

Each evening after supper, Alex sat at the aquarium for hours. When he removed the cover, some of the crickets would leap out, sticking to his shirt, his hair, his face. He fingered the stiff, spurred back legs, bent at forty-five degree angles, set for springing. He tapped the dark, hard shields on their backs, stroked the antennae, feathery ferns sprouting from each head.

He began to work the words *ovipositor, tarsus, thorax,* and *tympanum* into daily conversation.

And then one night, the crickets began to sing. In the darkness, as the boy slept and dreamed, hundreds of male forewings began to stir and resonate in the glass box. At first, a few, tentative notes sounded, the tuning of bows and strings. Then the confident, dissonant roar.

Across the hall, Robert and Sara listened.

Still awake at midnight, Robert said, "Listen Sara. They have individual voices, different pitches and tones. I detect vibrato in one of the tenors."

Sara moaned and rolled over.

At one a.m., Robert said, "If you count the number of chirps one cricket makes in ten seconds, multiply by six, and add thirty-two—that's the temperature. I read that once in *The Farmer's Almanac*." He rolled toward his wife, who was on her back staring at the ceiling. "It's seventy-four degrees in here."

Sara laughed. Robert, encouraged, slid his hand inside her panties, felt the smooth silk against the back of his hand, her warm wetness like a tongue on his fingertips.

Insomniaforeplay, they called it. A noun.

They made love.

At three a.m., Robert sat up in bed. "Those goddamn crickets are driving me nuts!" He shook Sara. "Did you hear me?"

"What am I supposed to do about it?"

The following afternoon, all of the crickets were dead. The boy discovered them that way after school, dry corpses in the grass, legs and antennae as brittle as old wire.

He cried and Sara hugged him warmly, letting his tears dampen the shoulder of her blouse. "Do crickets sing right before they die?" he asked.

"Apparently, honey," she answered.

She had used nearly a full can of insecticide, coating each of the shells with a clear, deadly glaze. The sweet, chemical odor still lingered in the room.

With his mother's help, the boy gave the crickets toilet burials, one by one at first, until she said, "All this flushing, we'll be in here all afternoon." After that, the crickets swirled down the toilet bowl by the handfuls, floating in a spiral on the surface, spinning faster and faster until they disappeared with each gurgling gulp.

Late home from work, Robert asked, "How did he take it?"

"How do you think?"

"He'll get over it. This weekend, we'll get him some goldfish or something."

"Goddamn you," Sara said.

That night, in the perfect quiet, Robert could hear his own blood thumping against his eardrums. Sara rested with her back to his, rigid, a hard shell curled like a boiling shrimp. From across the hall, he could hear Alex twitching, tapping a bare foot on the wall, rolling over and over, perhaps afraid of singing out in his sleep.

Then, from somewhere hidden, in a closet, perhaps, or under a cup-board, a lone cricket began to sing. An irregular song, uncertain, tenta-tive, with no steady volume or pitch.

Robert heard Alex stop twitching, heard nothing but the sound of listening coming from the boy's room. And beneath the sheet, like a stick of butter melting in a saucepan, Robert could feel Sara's body relax. He smiled. Slowly, like a man accepting a dare, Robert rolled over. Gently, he slid an arm over her ribcage. Cupped a hand around a warm breast.

Left it there.

Ten Things I've Heard
that I Believe

1. There was a young woman, a heroin addict, dying of AIDS in New York City. She didn't have any insurance so she was dying in one of those hospices, and a gay male nurse was caring for her. She was so weak she could hardly speak. Bedsores oozed like soft bruises on her back, and those black spots—Kaposi's sarcoma—dotted her chest and face. Her nurse was named Francesco or Francisco, something like that, and every night he held her hand and read to her from Whitman's Leaves of Grass to help her fall asleep—Whitman and morphine. A few hours before she died she asked Francesco to make love to her. Francesco smiled at her, kissed her on the forehead, and went into another room. He looked at a porn magazine, took off his clothes, wrapped himself in a bedsheet, put on a condom and some lubricant, and went into her room. She was lapsing in and out of consciousness when he got there. But he gently picked her up, rolled her airy body on top of his, careful not to dislodge the feeding tube or the I.V., and made love to her. Two hours later, as she died, she said she'd dreamed she'd been in the loving arms of God.

—Jennifer Rodick

"The stories we tell say a lot about us. The stories we *believe* tell us more." Every semester, for nearly fifteen years, Dave Robbins began his undergraduate American Folklore course with the same opening statement. He had it memorized, along with the rest of that opening day lecture, and he had to whip himself up with three or four cups of strong coffee and a wake-up aria of "Dr. Pepper's Lonely Hearts Club Band" in his office to walk into the lecture hall with any degree of enthusiasm, to offer that sea of dull young faces their money's worth. American Folklore was not a required class. But each semester, its seventy-five slots filled quickly, while other courses, History Department standards such as Western Civilization and The American Revolution, had open seats. Dave Robbins wasn't so vain to believe he was the only reason the course was so popular. As a comic or entertainer might acknowledge, he had good material. Historical mythology provided much of it, of course: George Washington's wooden teeth were driven like spikes into his gums and jawbone (not true); Ben Franklin flew a kite during a thunderstorm and was almost electrocuted (again, not true: he most likely made his son do the dirty work while he watched from a window, safely dry and warm, in the house); Pocahontas rescued John Smith's neck from the chopping block by stopping her father Powhatan's falling axe (never happened). The rest—and that was quite a lot of material—came from his students.

Dr. Robbins lets us participate in class. We aren't expected to sit like mindless sponges and soak up all that boring shit like we are in all our other history classes. We get to talk and tell stories about things we've heard.

Often, Dave Robbins had to fight to stay focused. You teach the same thing over and over, and inevitably, it becomes rote, like a chanted prayer. This semester, already weeks underway, had become especially difficult for him. He wandered about the front of the lecture hall looking for lost thoughts in the cracks of the faux marble, asbestos-laden tile. He paused in the middle of sentences, forgot the punch lines to his favorite Ronald Reagan jokes. He could sense his students growing restless, yet he couldn't find the spark to bring them back. He knew the reason: two small lumps on the inside of his right thigh. They were small peas under the skin when he first discovered them, a couple months earlier, wiping with a towel one morning after a shower. Now, they were both elongating, spreading and almost dividing, like peanuts in the shell, becoming four lumps instead of two. If he lectured with his hands in his pockets, he could feel them. Certainly by now, some students in the front row must have concluded he played with himself while he talked ("pocket pool" as a colleague called it). Sometimes, he tried to believe that the lumps were gone, or that they weren't really growing, that he only imagined them getting larger. But his imagination could not erase the proof he felt with the tips of his fingers.

~

The primary student project in American Folklore each semester was called the folklore journal. Students in the class had to keep a journal, noting each time they heard something they recognized as folklore, that is, some belief, saying, custom, or legend which has been passed down from one generation to another. Like the Greeks, Dave told them, who passed on Daedelus and Icarus, and many other myths, Americans had developed their own mythologies. He encouraged his classes to find them, and provided his students with a useful way of testing whether their entries were history, folklore, or, as he called it, fluff. If it's history, he said, it might appear in a history book. If it's fluff, you might read it in the *National Enquirer* or some other tabloid. If it's in between, it's probably folklore. Calling it folklore doesn't mean it's true and it doesn't mean it's false, he told them. It means only that it's important enough for somebody to remember and pass on.

2. *During the Civil War, three young friends from Georgia enlisted in the Confederate Army. They each carried a small sack of Georgia peaches with them, and they saved the peach pits as good luck charms when the peaches were gone, kept them in their trouser pockets and fingered them from time to time, when they grew homesick. All three of the men, they were boys, actually, only fourteen or fifteen years old, died in battle, on the banks of the Bull Run River. The boys and their clothes rotted there in the mud, and when the rains came, those peach pits sprouted in their pockets, sent tender shoots up through their bodies. Their young flesh and blood and bone became nourishing nitrogen, and iron, and phosphorous. And today in Manassas, Virginia, you can see where three small groves of peach trees have grown among the red pines, living memorials to three young confederates from Georgia.*

—Stephen Nickson

By the end of each semester, students were required to have at least ten items of American folklore listed in their journals, followed by a thorough analysis of their sources, the possible origins of the tradition, belief, or story, and a discussion of its value to American culture. Proper documentation of all facts and sources was absolutely necessary. Dave Robbins expected his students' folkore journals to adhere to the same rigorous, scholarly standards as his books did. He collected these journals every two or three weeks, to make certain each student was making progress. He wrote his comments, in green pen so they could distinguish his writing from their own, and returned them. Eventually, students learned that they could write notes to him in their journals, could ask questions, make comments, solicit opinions.

What's wrong with you? You seem out of it lately. Want to talk about it?
　　　　　　　　　　　　　　　　　　　　　—Jennifer Rodick

I *am* feeling out of it lately, Jennifer, nice of you to notice.
　　　　　　　　　　　　　　　　　　　　　　　　　—D.R.

In the waiting room of the oncologist's office, he paged through a *People* magazine, looked at pictures of venomous cobras and masturbating monkeys in *National Geographic*, and was just reaching for a copy of *American Heritage* that an old man with a bad toupee had been hoarding since he arrived when the nurse called him.

"So you have lumps," the good doctor said, glancing at Dave over his clipboard and the top of his glasses. Nude under a paper gown open in the back, Dave was staring at the jar of wooden tongue depressors and thinking about the Brazilian rain forests.

"On my thigh," he said.

"Show me."

A biopsy was scheduled for the following morning.

～

The next afternoon, Dave limped into the lecture hall fifteen minutes late, wincing as the twelve stitches in his thigh strained against his skin. He counted more empty seats than usual, but went on with the discussion.

3. *My grandma told me this story. In 1956, a man named Elmer Galik lived all alone in a small cabin in Moquah, Wisconsin, a tiny Slovak-settled town near Lake Superior. Everyone called his house the Bachelor's Cabin, because Elmer was a bachelor all his life. People always*

tried to set him up with women no one else would marry, women people called "second wives," because no one but widowers would consider them for wives, and then not until they were older, when beauty didn't matter so much. Elmer never dated any of them. One afternoon, when my grandma was sitting at the kitchen window, she heard a loud explosion, and she saw Elmer Galik's sad eyes flying past the window. Elmer had sat down on a case of dynamite and set it off. There was nothing left of his cabin but a charred black spot, and everyone said Elmer killed himself because he couldn't find a woman he wanted to marry.

—Julie Johanik

A whole category of folklore had emerged in America that focused on bachelors and old maids. This was the subject of class that afternoon. Inevitably, such folklore concerned murder, or suicide, or mental disease (sometimes all three), and used heterosexual loneliness as a motive to explain the behaviors. Today, Dr. Robbins said, with the openness and greater acceptance of homosexuality, this folklore is no longer used as often to try to force young men to find female companions, and vice versa. He looked up at the class, but could tell things weren't going well. Every time he put weight on his right leg and winced, he lost them. Even his best material of the day, the story of Ed Gein from Plainfield, Wisconsin, the 1950s graverobber, murderer, and cannibal who wore women's skin and danced around in the moonlight, who had a human heart in his frying pan when the authorities arrested him, failed to bring them to life.

Then, as class was dispersing, a question caught their attention. "Why are you a bachelor, Dr. Robbins?" It was Jennifer Rodick, sitting in the front row in tight bluejeans with her legs apart.

"Because I never married," he said, to groans of disappointment. "Class dismissed."

I'm sorry if I offended you with my question yesterday. I thought maybe you wanted to get personal, you know, that's kind of your teaching style. I didn't mean to imply that you're gay. Even if you are it doesn't matter, you're a good teacher, right? What happened to your leg? Can I cook dinner for you?

—Jenny Rodick

Ms. Rodick, why don't we go out for Chinese instead? About an hour after class on Thursday?

—D.R.

4. During World War II, in a French village under attack by the Germans, a farm girl ran into a small farmhouse to hide under a table. Her parents had been killed. An American GI saw her go into the house, and left his battalion to save her. He successfully ran through enemy fire, and as he reached the door, a shot rang out and the bullet pierced his groin, shattering one of his testicles. In great pain, he crawled to the woman, only to discover that she, too, was badly wounded. A bullet was lodged in her belly. After the battle, they were both taken to hospitals, and the woman wrote the GI's address on the back of his picture, so that someday she could write him to thank him. Months later, the woman went to her doctor, and discovered she was pregnant. When she told him it was not possible, (C'est impossible!), the doctor smiled and nodded. He said the virgin birth had been done before, read the Bible. But she was pregnant, and she delivered a healthy baby boy, nine months to the day after she'd been wounded. She figured it out. She looked at the picture of the American GI, and she could see the face of her newborn child. The same bullet must have passed through him and into her, carrying his sperm to fertilize her egg. She wrote to him to explain, and after the war, they fell in love and were married.

—Spence Taylor

Dave Robbins didn't date his students. He considered it unprofessional, unethical, and, inevitably, intellectually frustrating. He had dated a former student once, a former graduate student at that, someone near enough his own age that he didn't have to explain every reference he made from the 1960s, as he did now in his classes. ("The 'Chicago Seven?' Is that a rock band?").

Dating colleagues had proven equally unsatisfying, but for other, vague reasons he could never quite name. Unattached academic women, Doug Lester, one of his male colleagues once said, were about as much fun as horseflies buzzing on a window. Divorced academic women, he said, were like horseflies toting chainsaws. Dave didn't view them that way at all. Most were just alone, and as interesting and confused and frightened as anyone else. Some, of course, were slash and burn hedonists who compensated for their corpse-like professional earnestness with wildly self-destructive private behavior.

Once, in fact, Dave nearly married a brilliant assistant professor in the Political Science Department. Carly ("no relation to Al") Capone, her name was. In the summer, she liked to take midnight drives in her M.G. convertible, dressed in lingerie, with opera blasting from the stereo. She would sit in Dave's bathtub with a glass of bourbon and recite the entire fifth chapter of John Stuart Mill's *On Liberty* by heart. She was denied tenure when her dissertation on Castro's revolution, *My Lover, Fidel Castro*, told in the first person from the point of view of a fictional prostitute, failed to find an academic publisher. (She'd laughingly discussed a series, focusing on facist or communist leaders: *My Lover, Benito Mussolini; My Lover, Josef Stalin*, etc.) Last he'd heard, Carly was an assemblywoman in her home state of Utah or Arizona or Colorado, one of those square states out West.

When Carly left town, Dave remained chained and tenured in his academic position. He retreated into his work, and found the academy to be an intellectually intoxicating but terribly lonely place, where cynicism was served strong, like espresso, and happy, heterosexual couples were treated as if they must be doing something wrong.

And then came Jennifer Rodick, this slender young woman with very short blonde hair and a boyish face, who wrote beautifully and seemed to censor nothing, whose aggression came without bitterness, and whose invitation to dinner came at the only time in the last five years in which he would have accepted.

"You look beautiful," Dave said, as they awaited their won ton soup and eggrolls. "But I don't know what you're doing here. You're a bright, interesting young woman. Surely you've got other things to do than eat dinner at a second-rate Chinese restaurant with a geezer like me." Whenever he went out with a woman, his wit abandoned him. Clichés spilled from his mouth like vomit.

"You're the most amazing man I know," she said. "You, Axl Rose, and Thoreau."

Dave laughed. "Rose is the rock star, right? Guns 'n' Roses?"

"That's right," she said.

"And Thoreau, he's the witty anarchist who lived in the woods."

She smiled. "And they're both single," she said. "Like you."

"If your father knew you were at a restaurant with your history teacher, he would cut off your tuition and come looking for me with a meat cleaver."

She shook her head vigorously and her silver earrings—shaped like the skeletons of two small fish, hanging head-down nearly to her shoulders—tinkled against the sides of her face. "My dad is fifty-two—older than you, I'll bet, and he's married to a woman half his age. How old are you?"

"I'm forty-four."

"See, I was right. My stepmother is twenty-five, just two years older than me." She tugged on the corner of her shirt, a white silk blouse with roses, unbuttoned to her sternum, and tucked into tight black jeans. "This is hers. We share clothes all the time. They live an hour away."

"I see," he said. "I guess you're right."

"Why are you so sad?" she asked. "You're so brilliant and you've got the gentle eyes of a beautiful little boy, but everyday I come to class and I look at you and it just breaks my heart. Really. Like you're not whole, or something." She reached across the table and touched his arm, just above his watch. Her fingernails were painted red, and one of them clicked against the crystal.

"I don't know," he said.

"I'll help you," she said. "You need me."

~

Dave soon discovered that Jennifer shared the upper floor of a duplex with two other girls, both of them fifth or sixth-year seniors, like her. They were both sitting on a dilapidated sofa watching PrimeTime Live on television, with open books on their laps, when Jennifer and Dave opened the door and walked into the kitchen. On television, Diane Sawyer was chasing a man with a hidden camera and a microphone, making that pouty mouth she makes when he refused to answer her questions.

"Hi guys, I'm back," Jennifer said.

"Hi," they said.

Jennifer walked into the living room and Dave followed awkwardly behind her. "You guys, this is Dr. Robbins, my folklore teacher."

"Call me Dave, please," he said, and shook their hands. The shorter one wearing a man's long-sleeve shirt and white sweatsocks, with the dirty outline of her feet on the bottoms, was named Holly. The other one was taller, with a rainbow of colors dyed into one side of her mane of wildly kinked blonde hair. Her name was Crystal. She fronted an all-female rock band/performance art troupe on campus called "Crystal and the Chandeliers." Crystal and Holly folded their books closed on their laps and disappeared, one after the other, into the bathroom, and then into their rooms.

"We have a system," Jennifer said, smiling. She turned the stereo on and tuned it to a jazz station. "In a flat this small, you have to have rules, a system. Don't worry. They won't come out of their rooms unless the stereo is off, not even to use the bathroom. They'll pee in plastic buckets if they have to."

~

It was inevitable that Jennifer would discover his stitches. Though they were protected by white hospital tape, they were hardly inconspicuous. They looked like loops of thin black wire under dirty cellophane. Blood had dried into the tape.

Reclined nude on Jennifer's bed, illuminated by the four or five candles flickering on her dresser, Dave tried to relax as she kissed her way down his stomach and ran one hand along his ribs. She had pinned a condom, still in its foil packet, to her hair with a roach clip. "No pockets," she had said, smiling.

"Oh God," she said, suddenly, covering her mouth. "You have stitches!"

"I should have told you."

"Well, shit, they're right *here* in the Magic Kingdom," she said. "I'd have to be blind to miss them. What happened?"

"Nothing happened," he said. "I had surgery. I had some lumps checked out."

"Oh my God," said Jennifer. "You're dying, aren't you. That's it." She sat up in bed, her body illuminated by dancing candlelight.

"I don't think so," Dave said. "I mean, I won't know for a few days. I don't want to think about it."

Jennifer sat crosslegged on the bed and stared at him.

"Don't worry," he said. "I won't die in here."

~

Later that night, after they'd been asleep for awhile, Dave felt her shaking him. "Wake up. I have to tell you something," she said. "Come on. It's important."

"What?"

She leaned over him earnestly. "That entry in my journal, about the woman dying of AIDS and the gay guy who makes love to her before she dies. I made it up. All of it. I want to be a screenwriter. I got the idea from that movie, *Kiss of the Spider Woman*, when Raul Julia lets William Hurt butt-fuck him even though Raul is a homophobe."

"That's dishonest," he said, immediately angry at himself for not stifling his teacherly impulse.

"I know," she said. "I'm sorry. But I've got news for you. People make up a lot of the stuff in those journals."

"Really?"

"Sure."

"What about the source analysis, the discussion of cultural relevance, the footnotes?"

"That stuff too."

"Really?" He felt stunned. Betrayed.

"Don't look so shocked," she said. "They only do it because they don't want to disappoint you. You're very demanding in there. Your brilliance challenges people. Believe me."

～

In the morning, Jennifer left early for class, and Dave tried to wait until the other girls left before getting out of bed. He didn't have to be on campus to teach until that afternoon. But by ten o'clock he figured one of them was never leaving, so he wandered out into the living room with his pants on and Jennifer's bathrobe wrapped around his shoulders.

"Morning, Dr. Robbins," Holly said.

"Dave," he corrected her.

"Right." She smiled. "Dr. Dave. There's coffee left there. Help yourself."

He poured himself a cup and stood behind the sofa, where Holly sat watching "Mothers Who Nag Their Overweight Daughters" on *Sally Jessy Raphael.*

In the daylight, Dave could plainly see that the flat was a mess. It pulsed with the clutter of these young women's lives. Dirty laundry piled in every corner. Shoes everywhere. Magazines—*Rolling Stone*, *Vogue*, *Cosmopolitan*, and *Time*—in stacks on the floor, on the television, stuffed between torn cushions on the sofa. Dishes soaking in brown water in the kitchen sink. The bathroom looked like a drug store after a wind storm, with open bottles of shampoo and conditioner, facial creams, hair mousse, hair spray, hair remover; make-up splattered in the sink; eye-liner; blush; open tubes of toothpaste; toothbrushes in the shower and on the sink; pantyhose hanging across the shower bar like shrunken leg skin; boxes of douche; open packages of sanitary napkins; and a coffee mug of tampons on the back of the toilet, the plastic applicators poking out like so many fountain pens.

He sat down on the sofa across from Holly and sipped his coffee. She was still wearing the man's shirt—her boyfriend's, undoubtedly—and the dirty white sweatsocks, and because she sat with her legs crossed Dave could see a hint of pink bikini panties.

"Holly," he said, "let me ask you something."

"Sure."

"What do you believe?"

"What do you mean?"

"Just that. If someone asks you what you believe, what do you say?"

"Do you mean like do I believe in God? in love? in the boogie man? What? That's an open ended question."

"Yes, Holly, it is."

"So I can say anything?"

"Anything."

She thought for a moment, scratching her toe as she did. Then she looked at him. "I believe," she said, "when I feel like shit, when my boyfriend Mike has just dumped on me and I'm failing chemistry for the third time, I crawl into bed with a huge bowl of candy corn and chocolate covered raisins, and a cup of hazelnut cream coffee, and I sip and eat and watch *Oprah*, and I feel a little better. Sometimes I think without Oprah, I couldn't make it through the day."

"That's it?" Dave said.

Holly shrugged. "I believe in a million things," she said. "But that's all I could think of right now. I don't think well under pressure. Especially when a professor wearing my roommate's robe is staring me in the face."

Dave looked down at the fuzzy yellow robe he wore over his shoulders. "Holly, do you believe science will ever find a cure for cancer?"

She shook her head. "No. Someone—I think one of my chemistry teachers—once said that searching for a cure for cancer was like looking for a thousand needles in a million haystacks. But I'm failing chemistry for a thousand needles in a million haystacks. But I'm failing chemistry so what do I know." She looked at him. "Now, let me ask you something."

"Fire away."

"Did you sleep with Jen?"

"Yes I did."

"Looks like she gets an A then."

Dave smiled.

"I hope you don't just dump her. Jenny's going through some bad shit right now. When her big sister died, she just lost it. Don't dump on her, okay?"

"Her sister?"

"Sure. You know about it. She said she wrote about it in your class. Her sister died of AIDS. She was quite a bit older than Jenny, major messed up on drugs and shit."

"Is that what she told you?"

"I went with her to New York for the funeral," Holly said. "Her sister looked like a skeleton, honest to God. They used thick make-up to cover up her skin tumors, but if you knew they were there you could still see them. Her best friend Francesco was there. He made a piece of that big AIDS quilt for her. They had it hanging behind the casket. I never saw so many gay people in one place in my life."

Dave sighed. "I thought she made that up."

"Shit no," Holly said. "Why would she do that?"

～

The oncologist called his office just before class.

"Mr. Robbins," he said, "this is Dr. Wahlberg, glad I caught you in."

Dave broke into a sweat. The doctor's voice was, he felt, upbeat, a good sign. He waited.

"I'm afraid we have some bad news. Would you like to come into the office? It's more helpful, I've found, for patients to be sitting with me for this."

"No," Dave said. His hands were shaking so badly he couldn't hold the phone steady. "I have a class. The phone is fine. I'm fine, really."

"Well, all right. We found a malignancy. I want to be honest with you anything to say.

"We can work up a treatment schedule eventually that will be mini-mally disruptive to your professional life. We'll need to do tests first, of course. If there is no metastasis, the prognosis could be very, very good." He paused. "Mr. Robbins?"

"I'm here," Dave said. "Yes, I hear you."

"We have some work to do. No need to get into all of this now, over the telephone."

"No, of course not, you're right," Dave said.

"I'm sorry it couldn't be better news. I'll put the receptionist back on the line and she can schedule your next few visits and your MRI."

~

He lost control in American Folklore.

"It has been brought to my attention that many of you have been using creative license in your folklore journals." There were many smiles and a few soft giggles. "Well, people, this is not a fiction class, so as of now that practice will stop. If you want to write fiction, join the Marxists over in the English Department."

Jennifer, sitting in her customary place in the front row, mouthed the word, "Bastard," and slammed her notebook.

"The study of folklore is not some fucking game. From now on, I want sources so well documented I can verify every word of your entries with a single phone call. I want honest, critical analysis of the cultural values you ascribe to your entries. I will no longer wink at creative bull-shitting, tossing it off as part of the learning process. If I read bullshit, I'll flag it."

A male voice came from the back of the hall, "It's all bullshit, Doc."

"What?"

"A grand illusion, man."

"That's it," Dave said, limping around the lecturn, waving his arms and wincing in pain. "Get the fuck out of here, all of you. I don't want you back until you're ready to be honest."

"What about you?" A woman's voice. Jennifer. "You hide from the mys-teries of your own life by analyzing everybody elses'."

"What about you?" A woman's voice. Jennifer. "You hide from the mysteries of your own life by analyzing everybody elses'."

A few shouts of "Yeah!" and "All right!" echoed behind her.

"I am not hiding," he said, his voice rising, "I am *teaching*, goddamnit."

"That's bullshit!" she countered. "You hide in your little office! You hide in your books! You're hiding now."

"The fuck I am!" he said.

"Why are you limping?" Jennifer shouted. "Tell us that. You be honest with us for a change."

"I'm limping, Ms. Rodick," he said loudly, approaching her, "because I had two malignant lumps carved from my leg."

"Malignant?" she said softly.

"I have cancer, goddamnit," Dave shouted, pounding a fist into the other hand with each word. "Satisfied with that honesty, you bunch of post-high-school, think-you'll-live-forever, Diet Coke-junkie twits? Now get out of my sight!" And like Richard III, he limped off the stage and never heard the stunned applause which greeted his emotional exit.

Dr. Robbins is one crazy dude but he's the only prof. I ever had who's REAL. I learned a hell of a lot in his class. I don't know if it was history or what, but it was cool.

5. We are losing the battle against cancer.

—Holly, Pre-med.

Two days later, Dave moved into the flat with Jennifer, Holly, and Crystal. When you have cancer, he decided, you can do anything you want to do. Jennifer showed him a picture of her sister Nancy, read him some Whitman, and they made love in her bedroom with the door open, while Holly and Crystal cooked a deep-dish pizza in the kitchen.

Dr. Wahlberg explained metastasis. He said picture a fifty-gallon drum of toxic waste dumped in a river. For awhile, it sits there. Maybe a little bit leaches out of a seal, and a few fish in the area die, but basically the drum is there, and if you take it out in time, the river will be okay. But after awhile, the drum starts to rust, the toxic waste starts to spread downstream, and unless you can find it all, remove most of it, and kill the rest with chemicals and radiation, the whole river dies.

"As far as we can tell," Dr. Wahlberg said, "we got the drum out after it started to rust. You have what is called metastasized adenocarcinoma. There are some spots on your liver I don't like. The cancer has also spread to the bone, in your hips, your spine. This type of malignancy is a real bastard, I won't kid you. We'll do some localized radiation, and we'll go after it with chemotherapy, try to beat it into remission. It won't be pleasant, but it can work."

"And if I say the hell with it?"

Dr. Wahlberg shrugged. "You've got six months. Maybe less."

6. *The Geneva Convention outlawed the use of chemical and nuclear weapons against soldiers in modern warfare, but American cancer patients were left holding the bag.*

—Dr. Neil Wahlberg

To prevent the unsightly molted look brought on by the radiation and chemotherapy Dr. Wahlberg would be prescribing, Dave Robbins shaved his head and started wearing a bandana. To complete the look, Holly and Jennifer held icecubes on each side of one of his earlobes for five minutes, after which Crystal drove a needle through it and then forced in an earring, a small diamond stud, the mate for which had long been lost.

When Doc Robbins started dressing like Little Steven from "Little Steven and the Disciples of Soul," students not even enrolled in his class started showing up, like the faithful on a pilgrimage to a shrine or something. Sometimes when I left that class, I felt like I was walking out of the most unbelievable movie I'd ever seen.

That night, Jennifer and Holly took him to a bar in the student union called "The Library" to hear Crystal's band. The bar was dark, noisy, and very crowded, but Crystal had saved them a table right in front of the stage. The Chandeliers were four young women, three guitarists and a drummer, and Crystal stood in front at the microphone wearing a nude body stocking with a steel wool pad pinned to her crotch for pubic hair.

"It took us an hour to get that thing pinned on right," Jennifer said to Dave, yelling in his ear. "She's being Eve, tonight. She's in this weird, characters-from-the-Bible stage. She went to her Milton class today dressed like Delilah. They were reading *Samson Agonistes*."

"She's a very interesting person," Dave yelled, nodding.

"She *kicks ass*," Holly screamed, apparently in agreement.

"Her between-set performance tonight is dedicated to you," Jennifer said, squeezing his arm.

That performance came up quickly. The other girls left the stage, and Crystal stood quietly, alone at the microphone in a single spotlight, all the students watching in anticipation. The drummer, a short, dark-haired girl wearing black lipstick and eyeshadow, handed her something with a long cord dangling from it. Crystal bent over to plug it in, then turned it on and held it, buzzing loudly, against the microphone. It was a barber's electric razor.

"Yul Brunner," she said.

Slowly, almost erotically, Crystal cut a swath of her hair from the middle of her head, giving her what might best be described, Dave decided, as a reverse mohawk.

"Sinead O'Connor," Crystal said again. She cut another swath clean to the scalp.

"Michael Jordan," she said, and cut again.

"Victims of the Holocaust. The Dalai Lama. Buddhist monks." She continued, reciting the name of some prominent person or people without hair before cutting off more of her own. Soon, she was standing in the light, completely bald, the bumps on her scalp shining like wet eggs. She turned off the electric razor, put her mouth to the microphone, and said, "Dr. David Robbins." The spotlight went out, and everyone in the bar started yelling and clapping and laughing.

~

"I've been hearing things, Dave." Dean Charlie Hansen leaned across the desk and stared hard at him. He had those thick, Andy Rooney eyebrows that tipped up at the corners like wings, and Dave stifled a smile.

"What are you hearing Charlie?"

"Rumors. I don't need the vice chancellor on my ass about this. The hair, the earring, all that other crap. What's going on? You having a midlife crisis? I'm hearing some really unbelievable crap here."

"Such as?"

"Such as you're living with three of your female students."

"Not true. Only one of them is my student, the others are friends."

"Oh, well," he threw up his hands, "my mistake. That makes it all right. Are you nuts? The female faculty are going to be scratching down my goddamn door about this."

"Scratch back, Charlie."

"You've heard of sexual harrassment, I assume," Charlie said. "And the Faculty Code of Conduct."

"I'm not harrassing her, I'm living with her," Dave said. "She's twenty-three years old. If somebody tried to harrass her she would kick his balls into his throat."

"And what about your folklore class? What the hell is going on in there?"

"We're searching for things to believe, Charlie. Like always."

"I'm hearing it's some kind of secular revival in there, that you're playing music so loud people can hear it outside of the goddamn building."

Dave smiled. "Must have been Woodstock week."

"Have you talked to Phil Stevens in Biology? He's pissed because he says students enrolled in his class are cutting it to go to yours across the hall. Are you letting students into your classes who aren't even enrolled in them?"

"Look Charlie," Dave said, "it's a pit class. It would take me a half hour to take role."

"I know, I know," Charlie said, holding up his hands. "We're friends, right? I mean we both have been here for awhile. You're a hell of a teacher. I know that, everybody knows that. Your teaching evaluations read like hero worship, for Christ's sake. Your books are first rate. But come on, just ease back a little bit for me, okay? This isn't the Dave Robbins I know. I mean, whatever's going on with you, be more private with it. That's all."

7. When good professors become administrators, someone injects them with something that turns their spines into yogurt.

—Doug Lester, Assistant Professor of History

Crystal, Holly, and Jennifer spent one afternoon papering the flat with the word, "REMISSION." It was written in grease pencil in the shower, in soap on the bathroom wall, in candle-wax on Jennifer's mirror. It was stenciled on the apartment door and on the refrigerator door. Written in lipstick on the inside of the toilet seat. Painted in blue letters a foot long on the ceiling of Jennifer's bedroom. Spray-painted on both sides of Dave's 1983 Toyota Corolla. Printed in pen on one hundred yellow post-it notes plastered nearly everyplace else.

"Psychological warfare," Jennifer said.

"Mind games," Holly said.

"You've got to think it to sink it," Crystal added.

"Thank you," Dave said. "Thank you. Thank you."

Living with these three young women, Dave felt as if he'd shed his old, scholarly life like a skin. Three days a week, for nearly fifteen years, he'd walked into a classroom of fresh, foreign faces, each year the same age, though he was another year older, to teach them what he knew about his specialized chunk of the academic world. After class, he never knew where they went, what they did, what they valued, how they lived. Living with Jennifer, Holly, and Crystal changed that. He'd forgotten how much everything *mattered* to the young; how parents, grades, and sex loomed as a constant, haunting specters in their consciousness; how friendships and loves were formed and nurtured with the delicacy of orchids, and lost with the devastation of floods; how they quoted popular music with the reverence Muslims held for Mohammed, and lived still believing in the axioms he had long ago dismissed: all you need is love; I'll get by with a little help from my friends; you can't always get what you want, but if you try sometimes, you get what you need.

8. Life doesn't come with footnotes and a bibliography.

—Crystal

In a month, after three chemotherapy sessions that felt like molten iron was being poured into his veins, sessions which left him angry, weak, and so sick his stomach felt like a sponge squeezed dry, Dave and Jennifer stopped having sex, though he continued sleeping with her in her bed. In part, they stopped being lovers because most days he was so exhausted that he could barely last until seven o'clock before falling asleep. In part, because he and Jennifer had become friends.

"It's just not there for you, is it?" she asked him.

"I'm sorry," he said.

"It's okay," she said. "I knew. I could tell. You were doing it for me, not for you. For a man to do that is unbelievable."

"It wasn't all that selfless," he said. "I like it. It feels nice for me, too, you know." These things were true. "It's the drugs, too. I just can't, anymore."

She hugged him and he could feel her crying.

9. *"Sex is like a nuclear bomb going off in your soul."*
                                   —Song lyric, Crystal and the Chandeliers

"Everything we're doing is the accepted procedure for battling this type of cancer, Mr. Robbins," said Dr. Wahlberg. "But so far, the tumors aren't responding."

"They aren't?"

Dr. Wahlberg shook his head. "I'm sorry, no."

"The tumors haven't shrunk at all?"

The doctor pursed his lips and shook his head again. "The spots on your liver have actually gotten a little bit bigger. Are you feeling any pain in your back?"

Dave felt angry, helpless, exhausted.

"We can still be optimistic," the doctor said. "It is still relatively early. It sometimes takes many months to show progress."

"How many months?"

The doctor shrugged. "Four. Six, maybe."

"And if it doesn't work by then?"

Dr. Wahlberg looked at him. "We can try something else," he said.

"Has anything else worked?"

Dr. Wahlberg shrugged. "Statistically, our success ratios with conventional treatment of this type of cancer have been low, with a five-year survival rate of about five to ten percent. Your odds probably wouldn't be any worse with unconventional therapy."

"What do you mean by unconventional? Coffee enemas? Avocado milkshakes? Quartz crystal teas? What?"

"I'm sorry," Dr. Walhberg said.

～

"Dave," said Dean Hansen, embracing him in that awkward, face-away hug men give one another when they are forced to. "Why didn't you say something? I have to hear this from students?"

"I'm sorry, Charlie," Dave said. Throughout his career, every time he apologized to the dean, he always wanted to add, "only good-tasting tuna get to be Starkist."

"Can we do anything for you? Do you need anything? Can we reduce your courseload, schedule some T.A.s to do your grading? What?"

"Nothing," Dave answered. "Really. I'm getting better."

"Really? That's great news! That's fantastic news."

～

The night before he moved out of Jennifer's flat, Dave Robbins dreamed that all of the students in his folklore class had come to take his final exam with their heads shaved. He looked out over the lecture hall and their heads glowed like imperfectly rounded crystal balls with ears. And behind him, written in white on the green chalkboard, were ten inspirational stories about people who had been cured of terminal cancers, spectacular medical miracles told in the hopeful, exclamation-marked prose one encountered in waiting-room copies of Reader's Digest. Beneath these stories were the names and phone numbers of their sources, for verification.

When he awoke, his spirits momentarily buoyed by that dream-induced hopefulness, Dave felt the crushing return to wakefulness. The flat was quiet. Jennifer, Crystal, and Holly were gone to class. He quickly showered, packed his clothes and books into boxes, loaded them into his car, and drove to his office.

Sitting at his office desk, with a desperation he'd seen in students writing final exams, he turned to the only thing he'd known to do to make the world meaningful. He wrote. He took a pad of paper from the drawer, and across the top he wrote, "Ten Things I've Heard That I Believe." He numbered the list down the left margin. He wrote with a fury, from memory, in the languages of his students, his colleagues, his doctor, until his hand cramped, until the fingers and thumb curled involuntarily toward his palm, claw-like. An hour passed. And another. He read and reread the first nine items on the list, silently, aloud while sitting at his desk, even louder while pacing the floor. Perfect, beautiful, incandescent.

"Ten," he said aloud, finally, to himself. He wrote:

"A history professor was dying of metastatized adenocarcinoma. Conventional therapy included localized radiation and chemotherapy, but the tumors did not respond to treatment. He got well anyway. No one could explain why."

He read it aloud to himself, over and over, as if by association with the other entries it would take on their power. Yet, each time he read it, his own voice sounded foreign. A lifetime of scrupulous observation and documentation had left him unprepared for this, this what—this *something* he couldn't quite articulate. In numbers one through nine, he found hope and wonder, the magical, though imperfect, collective mythology of American life, words to cherish, to live and die for, to have and to hold, to believe.

But number ten was a fiction. He could read it aloud a million times, and he could not, with his voice, transform it into fact.

So he held the list in one hand and struck a match.

He watched as the paper curled away from the heat of the tiny flame and then caught fire, the flames slowly spreading along the edges, creeping toward his hand. When the flame flared toward his face, Dave dropped the burning list into the metal wastebasket next to his desk. The other paper inside caught fire, and for minutes the wastebasket belched smoke and flames, the wispy ashes rising on the heated air before they cooled and fell to the floor, as useless as the wings of Icarus.

The Summer I Learned Baseball

WE WERE DRIVING to Madison to buy a new car from one of Daddy's former teammates. Daddy never did anything that didn't pertain to baseball in some way.

"This car smells like piss," Rosie whined, her nose pinched closed as she slouched in the back seat, behind Mama. Her dirty knees were pressed against the seat back, her bare feet dangling above torn tennis shoes. Because she was the youngest, she always got to sit on the 'good' side where the springs were still coiled safely beneath the upholstery. On my side, the sharp points had punctured the dirty vinyl in rows, leaving tiny holes rimmed with rust, so I was allowed to sit on the Sears Christmas Catalog, which made me taller. I had to duck whenever Daddy wanted to see through the rear view mirror. Babe, at fifteen the oldest and tallest, sat silently in the middle with her arms crossed, ducking for no one.

"What's that, honey?" Daddy called back to Rosie. It was hard to hear anything in that car. Daddy was driving fast, and the wind was a rush in our ears. Also, the car had no muffler, and the quarter panels were so rusted they flapped like hummingbird wings.

"I said: THIS IS A PISSY CAR!" Rosie shouted. It was 1978, and we owned the only 1964 Chevrolet in Waushara County, Wisconsin.

"Ah, but it's a WONDERFUL world," Daddy shouted back. He was always saying things like this to make it up to us. The car really did smell.

"It's the cat," I said. "He RELIEVES himself in here."

"Well, chase him out Ty," Mama said. She was holding the hair down on both sides of her head, but some of it swirled across her face and mouth. All of the windows were wide open, it being late August, and sticky. I had no choice: my window was lost inside the door somewhere, off the track. Without the dirty glass between me and the world, I saw everything clearly. Field mice had built a nest under the back seat. One morning I had watched their squeaking, pink babies pulled out one at a time by one of our tomcats, who ate them like shrimp cocktail.

"Sonny, you should have fixed that back window," she said.

Daddy laughed.

The mice came in through the holes in the floorboard. Under my feet were two pieces of soiled cardboard cut from a produce box, which covered two holes nearly as big around as a baseball. Baseballs were always rolling around the floor of our car, and one almost fell out before Daddy covered the holes. If it hadn't been for Daddy's fear of losing one of his precious baseballs, one of his children might have fallen through the floor of the car before he would have done anything about it.

"Tell us again, Daddy," Rosie said. "Tell us about the car we're going to buy."

"Well, it's a glittering goddess," he began, "a gift from Detroit fit for a home run king, with chrome so clean you can comb your hair in it. And under the hood," he smiled, "under the hood are two hundred and eighty horses drinking gas at three bits a delicious gallon. That's right, and inside you've got your AM and FM radio—standard. Your tinted glass—standard. Your automatic transmission—"

"STANDARD!" Rosie shouted.

"Right! And your carpeted floors and beautiful REAL cloth upholstery—"

"STANDARD!"

"And your refrigerating air conditioning—"

"STANDARD!"

"No! It's extra, but worth every penny to keep your mother's pretty hair from blowing out to leftfield."

"What color is it?" Rosie asked.

"Ah, baby, it's Dodger blue," Daddy said. "Blue like a June, baseball sky."

"Sonny, how are we going to afford this?" Mama asked him. "Who's going to loan us the money?"

"Don't you worry about that," Daddy said.

"Even if we get a loan," Mama said, "how we going to make the payments?"

"I tell you what," Daddy said. "We'll take a vote. Whoever earns the money in this car and wants a new one, raise your hand." Daddy raised his hand. "There you go." He looked at Mama. "Think of it, Deary. Automatic transmission. Air conditioning."

"Those are wonderful things," Mama said. "But we can't afford a new car, Sonny. You know that."

The back of Daddy's neck turned red, and in the mirror I could see the blue veins bulging like tangled vines on his forehead, below the rim of his baseball cap. His anger rose quickly, we knew. Beneath the mask of calm smiles and pretty words bubbled deep, troubled waters.

"Woman, don't you dare work against me on this," he snapped.

"Big man," said Babe, suddenly.

My face smashed against the back of the seat when Daddy hit the brakes and stopped the car. Rosie slid to the floor.

Daddy had his right finger pointed at Babe's face, and his hand was shaking. Babe looked scared, but she raised her eyebrows and stared at Daddy, waiting. Rosie whimpered.

"Just forget it," Babe said. "Let's just go get the stupid car. It's hot."

Daddy gripped the wheel with both hands and jammed his foot on the gas. The muffler roared and the quarterpanels flapped as the car sputtered back up beyond the speed limit. Babe grabbed Rosie by the back of the shirt and pulled her into her seat. Slowly, the blood drained from Daddy's neck, and the blue veins in his forehead flattened and disappeared.

"Brakes are still good," Daddy said to Mama, and chuckled.

Babe looked at me and rolled her eyes.

～

I was born the year Daddy quit playing baseball. 1966. Mama said he probably never would have stopped playing if he hadn't had a son. She said my coming along saved them all, because Daddy wasn't making enough money for food playing baseball, traveling around Texas in a minor-league bus, her home alone raising Babe. When he had a son, she said, he could play the game at home, get it out of his system.

They met when Daddy was a high school baseball star, an all-state third baseman who could gobble up those bullet groundballs, what Daddy called worm-shavers, with ease, a switch-hitter who could hit to both fields, bunt if needed, steal a base or two. He played professionally for nine years, just Class A ball mostly, though in 1963—his best year—he hit .253 with a triple, four doubles, and a home run in a half-year in double A, or so I'd been told at least one hundred times. He never made the majors and attributed it to many things, but mostly to his name: Jack "Sonny" Smith. It wasn't a name a manager was likely to remember, he said, not like Warren Spahn or Hammerin' Hank Aaron or the Yankee Clipper, Joe DiMaggio. So he named his firstborn child Babe after Babe Ruth, even though it was a girl. Rosie's full name is Rosetta, for Pete Rose. He named me Ty, after Ty Cobb. "That son-of-a-bitch was the greatest hitter the game has ever seen or will see," he said. But I couldn't hit a baseball if you dangled it in front of me on a string.

Not that Daddy didn't try to teach me.

Each birthday I'd get a wooden bat that was a little longer, a little heavier, than the year before, with promises that when I grew up I'd receive the major league bat which hung above the dresser in his bedroom, the one he'd used to hit his only professional home run. The wood had yellowed and dried out over the years, but Daddy always treated it with special reverence, and I was expected to treat it the same way. He put a new coat of clear finish on that bat every year. When thunderstorms rumbled through the county and the radio crackled tornado warnings, we'd rush into the crawlspace beneath the trailer, and Daddy would join us a minute later, cradling that wooden bat in his arms.

I was not gifted with a bat or a glove, and my right arm was incapable of throwing the ball hard enough to make the leather of Daddy's glove snap when he caught it. He'd toss soft pitches to me as I stood against the back of the trailer, bat in hand, but more often than not I'd swing and miss and the ball would bounce off the trailer and roll halfway back to him. Then he'd throw the ball and I'd miss it again, and he'd pull down the brim of his cap.

"Why don't I hit you some pop-ups," he'd say, and I would stand in the field off the back yard, pounding a fist into my glove, smelling the leather and the mink oil Daddy had worked into the pocket. At the crack of the bat the ball would rise, spinning, the seams hissing in the air, and then would turn in a gentle arc and fall. If the ball came right to me I caught it, amazed to see it nestled in my glove like an egg in a nest, but usually it would bounce in front or behind me, or thump off my chest, my wrist, or my head. "When you're older," Daddy'd say, as we walked back to the trailer, "you'll surprise yourself."

Sometimes on my bike I would carry his lunch to the building supply store where he worked, and he would eat as he walked me through the lumber yard, pointing to pieces of hardwood that would make the best baseball bats, or we'd sit down on a pile of two-by-fours, and he'd retell stories I'd heard dozens of times. "Son," he'd say, "without the Game you and I wouldn't be sitting here. God made this world with one big, home run swing." He'd wink and point at me. "Now, a priest will tell you different, but what's he know about baseball, right? Devil threw his best pitch and God took that big old God-bat, swung it like this—" he extended his arms in a slow-motion swing, his forearms bulging like the meaty end of a bowling pin "—and POW! he knocked this old earth spinning into heavenly orbit. Hit it so hard it ain't yet even coming down."

"The world's a baseball," I would say, doubtfully, dutifully.

"Hell yes it is!" he'd say, smiling. "The Rocky Mountains are just a big pile of dirt covering one of the seams, and the Alps cover the other. You take a shovel and you dig deep enough, you'll find the red string holding the cover of this old earth together."

"And the oceans?"

Daddy would wink. "That's what makes it special. That's what really makes it amazing," Daddy'd say. "The devil threw God a spit-ball, and He hit it out of the park."

As I grew older, I stopped sitting long enough for Daddy to finish his stories. I refused to join Little League even though he coached a local team, and eventually he stopped asking me to play catch, or to hit a few to him.

After work sometimes, Daddy'd go out alone in the yard by himself and hit a bucket of baseballs into the field. Mama would look imploringly at me. "Play with him, Ty," she would say. "You're all he's got."

But I remember thinking, how can a grown man let his life be ruined by baseball?

～

The Chevrolet dealership in Madison looked like a parking lot filled with new cars. It was hard not to be excited about it, all that glass and chrome shining. In the cool showroom we met the salesman. He was a former baseball player who made it to the majors for two years. Daddy called him "Red." "Utility infielder. Played with the Cardinals," Daddy said, "next to Lou Brock, the greatest base stealer the game has ever seen." We all nodded appropriately. You could see that Daddy admired the man. "Baseball opened a lot of doors for me," Red said, opening the door of a Cadillac that was in the showroom. Only Daddy laughed. He saw baseball as a fraternity of men who viewed the world in the same way.

On the lot, the salesman led us to the car that Daddy had picked out, a 1979 Chevrolet Caprice Classic. It was beautiful, long and sleek and blue, with whitewall tires, wire wheel covers, a hood ornament shaped—Daddy pointed out—like an umpire's chest protector.

"Here," the salesman said, handing Daddy the keys, "take it for a test drive. Baby rides like a rising fastball. With that power steering, you can turn a corner with one finger."

Sitting inside that car was like being in a new world. The seat was soft and plush, a royal blue velour, and you couldn't even feel the bumps on the road. With the windows up and the air conditioning on, I could even hear myself breathing. Daddy turned on the radio, and the smooth sound echoed from behind my head and in front of me.

"Quadrophonic stereo," Daddy said, and turned it off. "Isn't that something?"

On the highway, all you could hear was the hum of the tires on cement. No one was speaking. The ride was so quiet, no one wanted to disturb it.

Mama said softly, "Sonny, it costs twice as much as you make in a year."

"Deary, come on," Daddy said, "I played ball with Red in the minors for a year and a half. Had trouble hitting the curve ball or he might still be with St. Louis."

"What does that matter?" Mama asked.

"It matters."

"It *is* a beautiful car," she said.

"Fills your heart up like a balloon, doesn't it?" Daddy said. "Like watching Mr. Spaulding disappear over the wall, then going into your home run trot nice and slow, circling the bags, feeling the warm sun on your face, hearing the cheers of the crowd."

"This is a GREAT car," Rosie said.

"I love it," I said. It was hard not to get caught up in the moment.

"Could you put the radio on again?" Babe asked.

"Did I hear something?" Daddy asked Mama. "Was that the silent one, speaking?"

"Come on, Daddy," Babe said, slapping him on the shoulder.

Daddy turned on the radio. He put on a country station, but the radio sounded so good that didn't even matter.

∿

Back at the dealership, we waited in chairs by the Coke machine while Mama and Daddy sat down at the salesman's desk to talk business. His desk was in a separate office, but we could see them through a large window. A screen had been placed in the glass on an angle, so that each of the squares, tipped on its point, looked like a baseball diamond. Daddy would have been proud that I noticed that. He smiled at us when the salesman sat down, and we watched anxiously as they talked. After a few minutes, Babe wandered away to look at brochures in a display by the window. Rosie got bored and followed her. I sat with my back to the glass, closed my eyes, and waited.

And waited.

An hour passed. I looked in the office and Daddy was pacing the floor. Mama was sitting with her knees together, holding her purse on her lap. Red was on the telephone.

Thirty more minutes passed. I heard the door to Red's office slam open, and I turned just in time to see Daddy rush past. He walked out of the showroom without looking at us, just passed between a new Chevette and a new Cadillac and headed into the sunshine.

Mama and Red came out of his office together.

"I'm terribly sorry," Red said. "Please try to make him understand that. The credit company is a separate division. There's nothing I can do."

Mama forced herself to smile. "I understand," she said.

"We really do have some beautiful used cars on the lot," he added. "You come back, we'll fix you up with something nice. I want to do right by you folks, I really do."

"We already have a used car," Mama said.

We heard Daddy pull up in our old car before we saw him. He appeared at the front window of the showroom, revving the engine. Clouds of blue smoke billowed from under the car. We all climbed in, slamming the doors behind us. The vinyl seats were hot. Daddy punched the gas so hard I hit my head on the back window as we roared out of the lot.

∼

No one said anything until we were out of the city, cruising the flatland north between fields of rippling, green corn.

"It's okay, Sonny," Mama said.

"Hell it is," Daddy said. He hit the steering wheel with the palm of his hand. "The HELL it is."

Halfway home, Daddy pulled over at a gas station and bought a twelve-pack of beer. Back on the highway, he rested one arm on the twelve-pack and steered with his left hand.

"This country's going to hell," Daddy said. "I mean it. When a decent, working man can't walk into a showroom and buy the car he wants, it won't be long before it's all over."

"We know you work hard," Mama said.

"Don't patronize me," Daddy snapped.

"We couldn't afford the car, Sonny," Mama said. "There's no shame in that."

Daddy glared at Mama and yelled. "Don't tell me what we can and cannot afford, goddamnit!" he said. "I won't hear it. We got a roof over our heads. No holes in our shoes. All the food we want. A color T.V."

"But Sonny . . ." Mama said.

"Just shut up," Daddy said. "We should be rich. Hell, we are rich. We got all the money we need."

"Hah!" Babe said. She shouldn't have said it, but she did. "We're poor white trash," she said.

Daddy jerked the car to the gravel shoulder and stopped. He glared in the rear-view mirror at Babe. "What was that?" he asked.

My stomach knotted.

"People say it," she said. "Kids at school."

"What do they say?"

Babe swallowed. "You heard me."

"And you believe them."

"We *are* poor," Babe said. "Pretending we're not doesn't change it."

Daddy spun in his seat and the back of his hand caught Babe flush in the face. Babe screamed.

"Sonny!" Mama shouted. Blood spurted from Babe's nose. When Rosie saw it, she started crying, a high-pitched, deafening wailing.

"Big man!" Babe shouted.

Daddy hit her again. This time he leaned over the seat, and he slapped Babe in the face with his palm. Babe covered her face with her hands.

"Sonny stop it!" Mama screamed. She turned in her seat, put her back to the door, and started kicking Daddy's side with her heels. The first kick caught him in the ribs, and he had to pull in his arm to defend himself. Mama kept yelling, "Stop it! Stop it! Stop it!" And each time, she kicked Daddy hard.

Daddy opened the car door and went out, then slammed the door behind him.

"Respect me, goddamnit," he shouted so loud his voice was hoarse. "Respect me."

Mama slid over in the driver's seat and shifted the car into gear.

"Mama, what are you doing?" I asked.

She didn't answer. Daddy kicked the car once, kicked my door and made me jump. Mama pushed down on the gas pedal and we roared away. Next to me, Babe and Rosie were crying. Babe was holding the front of her shirt against her nose, and it darkened where the blood soaked in.

"Babe, you okay?" Mama asked.

Babe nodded.

We drove the rest of the way home in silence. Mama parked the car in the gravel out front of the trailer and left the beer on the front seat. We went inside, ate supper. Darkness came. We sat together in the living room, and waited.

"Ty, lock the front door," Mama said. "Babe, you get the back one."

We did as we were told, and returned.

"Your father's not a bad man," Mama said. "He's got a temper like a hive of bees, but he's got a lot of honey in him, too. Can't get one without the other in most men."

"Why's he have to lie about everything?" Babe asked. "He knows we're poor."

"That's your father," Mama said. "Ever since I've known him, he could talk himself into believing anything. Even has me going most of the time."

"Are we poor?" I asked. It really bothered me to hear Babe say that. I had never heard anyone in our family say it.

Mama looked at me. "We aren't rich," she said. "Put it that way."

～

We went to bed at ten o'clock, and there was still no sign of Daddy. All the windows were open. Through the screens, we could hear the buzz of crickets in the fields, the sound of cars passing on the highway, farm dogs barking in the distance. Rosie and I shared a bedroom, and after she fell asleep, I knelt on my bed, my elbows on the windowsill, waiting and watching for my father. But after an hour passed, I went back to bed and fell asleep.

Just after midnight, I was awakened by a loud noise. I heard it a second time and sat up. Daddy was back. He had kicked in the front door. I pretended to sleep as he came down the hall. The floor creaked as he went into Babe's room. I heard Babe's bed squeak when Daddy sat down on it, then I heard both of them whispering. After a minute or so, Daddy stood back up and walked into the hall, past our room, then into his own room. I heard him kiss Mama. When he emerged from the room, he was carrying his baseball bat. He took it back down the hall, through the kitchen, and outside. I half expected him to ask me if I wanted to catch some pop flies, but he didn't. He walked past my room and kept going.

I sat up in bed and watched. Outside, Daddy walked to the car, leaned the baseball bat against the front bumper, then opened the passenger-side door. In the moonlight, I could see his shirt was unbuttoned and soaked with sweat. His baseball cap was backwards on his head. He pulled the twelve-pack of beer from the front seat, set it on the hood, and tore the box open. He drank the first beer quickly, chugging it down and then squeezing the empty can before dropping it on the ground. He sat down on the hood and reached for another beer. Then another.

~

Sometime later, after I'd grown bored watching him drink, Daddy slid off the car to his feet. He looked at his prized baseball bat, picked it up, and took a few practice swings. He had a good, minor-league swing—compact, consistent, and powerful. Each time he swung, the barrel of the bat moved in a perfect parabola across the front of his body and thumped against his back.

Daddy squared his shoulders in front of the car and raised the bat over his shoulder, as if there were an imaginary pitcher standing on the trunk.

I held my breath and watched, astonished.

With the first swing, he drove the end of the bat through one of the headlights, shattering the glass and knocking the metal frame across the yard. Even though I expected it, the sudden noise startled me.

Rosie stirred. "What was that?" she asked.

"Daddy's home."

Daddy moved to the other headlight, took the same tight, powerful swing, and popped it like a glass balloon. Rosie jumped off the bed and ran to Mama's room.

Daddy circled the car with his baseball bat resting on his shoulder. He shattered the windshield with two fully extended home run swings, destroyed the windows on the passenger side, then the rear window. With each swing of the bat, glass exploded into the car and sprinkled the gravel driveway. The sound echoed off the trailer, but between swings, the world was reverently still. In the distance, even the dogs had stopped barking.

Babe, Mama, and Rosie came into my room. Mama pulled the curtains back and the four of us watched together, our faces framed by the window casing.

"Is he drunk?" Babe asked.

Mother shrugged.

When Daddy hit the driver's-side mirror, it popped high into the air, its square, chrome casing spinning and flashing in the moonlight, then clattered to rest on the roof of the trailer. He pivoted one-hundred-eighty degrees—my father the switch-hitter—and dented the door with a crushing left-handed swing. He raised the bat over his head and with a loud grunt caved in the roof. With a staccato flurry he peppered the hood. He paced. Raspy breaths heaved from his open mouth. Every few seconds he squared himself and brought the thick barrel of wood hard against the car in explosive, alliterative strokes. Sometimes he swung so hard he fell down, but he would curse, get back to his feet, to swing even harder the next time. Each time he connected, splinters of wood flew from the bat.

Watching Daddy then, something started happening to me. Beneath my pajamas, I could feel sweat trickling down my back, between my shoulder blades. The muscles in my body tensed. Every time Daddy hit the car, I sensed my own shoulders turning, my own wrists breaking in perfect rhythm. I shifted my weight from right foot to left, felt the sting of the wooden shaft vibrating in my hands. Like the pulse of new blood, I felt the wonder and glory of God's creative power surging in my skinny, school boy arms.

That summer, I learned to play baseball.

Women in the Woods

THE GIRL'S BODY rested face down, her blonde hair a mossy tangle of leaves and dirt, her skin coated with the white, crystalline fuzz of morning frost. The wire holding her crossed hands behind her back had cut into the flesh of her wrists, and small, round scars marked her buttocks. The sleeve of a white blouse was knotted behind her neck. Her toenails had been painted the candy-apple red popular with teenaged girls.

John Andrews stared at the body for a long time before he left the girl to find a telephone.

After hunting most of the morning, John had climbed down from his tree stand with his compound bow and arrows and had walked through a small stand of pines toward the county road where he'd parked his pick-up truck. His toes were numb after three hours of sitting in the below-freezing temperatures, and the walk warmed him, loosened his stiffened hips and knees. As a younger man, he could sit in a tree all day waiting for deer to pass beneath him, but now, after a few hours, he was so stiff it was a trick to return to the ground without falling.

Halfway to the road, he'd cut fresh deer tracks in the snow and had followed them through the stubble of a cornfield into the swamp. He found the girl's body in a tangle of flattened cattails and marsh grass. The deer he was following had circled the body before bounding into the safety of the thick brush.

That's what John told the police dispatcher when he called from Elmer Franklin's house. Now nearly eighty, Elmer was a friend of John's father, and John had been hunting on his farmland since he was a boy. Within minutes of the telephone call, three police officers, the county sheriff and a deputy, a homicide detective, and two paramedics in an ambulance, had joined John and Elmer on the Franklins' ice-strewn, gravel driveway. After handshakes and terse introductions, the men crossed the highway into Elmer's cornfield, their breath clouds of steam in the icy air. One deputy, a young man named Buddy, stayed back in the sheriff's car with the engine running.

"Shit it's cold," one of the men said as they walked, single file, across the cornfield, with John and Elmer in the lead.

"Wind chill minus five," one of the paramedics said. He was carrying a canvas stretcher, and the canvas flapped in the wind against his leg. The other paramedic carried a black body bag folded beneath his arm.

"Pussies," the detective said. "This is nothing." He was a large man who struggled to keep up at the end of the line. He carried a small, black suitcase in one hand and a paper cup of coffee in another. He tried to walk and drink his coffee at the same time, but gave up and threw the steaming cup on the ground. "I've seen it so cold it would freeze your dick if you pulled it out of your pants. Freeze up so hard you could drive a nail with it."

The paramedics laughed.

"I'm not kidding," the detective said. "This is nothing."

When the men reached the woods, they stepped over a sagging stretch of rusted barbed wire, passed through the stand of white pines, and came to John's footprints in the snow.

"These your tracks?" the sheriff asked him.

"Yes, sir," John said. Then he added, "Officer." He felt embarassed calling a man obviously younger than him, "sir," but wasn't certain "officer" was any better.

"Call me Bill," the sheriff said.

"O.K."

"Don't see any other tracks here," he said. "Only yours. So you say you were over there," he gestured through the pines to the hardwoods, where John's deer stand was located, "and you passed through here on your way to your truck." He turned and pointed to the truck, which was at a right angle to the path John had taken. "But your truck's over there."

The implication shocked, and then angered, John. He had no reason to be nervous, but he found himself answering defensively. "I *was* on my way home," John said. "But I cut fresh deer tracks, and they led in here."

"Okay," the sheriff said, and gestured with his arm that they should proceed.

The thump of their boots and shoes on the frozen ground beneath the snow resumed until the girl's body appeared before them. John stopped about ten feet from her, and the others stopped behind him. To his surprise, he saw that his previous boot tracks stopped only inches away from the body.

"There she is," John said.

"I'll be damned," the detective said, as if he didn't believe John had really discovered a body.

Elmer tried to step closer, to get a better look, but one of the police officers held his arm.

"Rope it off," the sheriff said, "and let's get started." He looked at Elmer and John. "You folks hang around here for awhile, if you don't mind. We'll have some questions for you. If it gets cold, we can do it later, at the station."

"Anything you need, officer," John said.

He said to Elmer, "We'll need a list from you of all the people who hunt on your land and everybody who knows you."

Elmer said, "Nobody I know would do this."

"We'll need the list of names, anyway," the sheriff said.

"Hey," the detective, a man the sheriff called Frank, said to John, "You didn't touch it, did you?" John looked at him. A wedge of fat bulged from under the detective's chin. His winter coat was unzipped, and his belly poked through it. There was a yellow mustard stain on his brown tie.

"No," John said. "No, I didn't touch her."

"Why'd you get so close?"

"I don't know," John said.

"Hard up to see a bare ass? Better than a nudie magazine?"

"Come on, Frank," the sheriff said to him. "This citizen found the body and reported it. Maybe he needed to get a closer look to make sure it was what he thought it was."

"Curiousity killed the cat," Frank said. He removed his leather gloves and pulled a pair of white latex surgical gloves from his pocket. He puffed his breath into each one and put them on.

Two of the police officers unrolled yellow ribbon and hung it in the underbrush in a circle around body. "POLICE LINE DO NOT CROSS" was written in black on the ribbon, which fluttered like crepe paper at a party.

The sheriff pulled his walkie talkie from his belt and turned it on. He put his mouth to it.

"Buddy, you with me?" he asked.

"Gotcha. What you need?"

"We got a female Caucasian here, a young one. Could be the Van Horn girl. Call dispatch and get the vitals for me, will you? I left the sheet on my desk."

"Gotcha."

When the police had completed their loop around the body, they began to walk methodically through the thick marsh grass, which reached to their armpits in places. The detective ducked under the ribbon and stood over the girl. He dropped his black case in the snow and tucked his tie into his shirt. Then he leaned over the body and talked softly into a tape recorder the size of a small flashlight.

"Looks like cigarette burns on her ass," the detective said. "Four, five, six of them. All third degree."

"What do you think, Frank?" the sheriff asked.

"She's dead," he said.

"Don't fuck around," said the sheriff.

"Give me a few minutes," he said. "I'm not a psychic for Christ's sake."

Elmer and John walked to the edge of the police ribbon and watched. John felt his legs shaking. Only now, after his part in the drama was over, was he feeling the revulsion and sickness that had not come when he discovered the girl's body. When he first saw her, from a dis-

tance, he thought she was a dead deer, the white belly swollen. He had
hit a doe a week earlier, had driven an arrow into her ribs, but had lost
the blood trail in the dark and had never found her. So this is where she
went to die, he thought to himself at first. But then he saw the feet, those
thin, perfectly human feet, with the red polish on the toenails, and the
stiff hands crossed behind her back. He had approached cautiously, had
known immediately that he had found something no one but one other
person had seen. He went close to the body, looked at it intently—even
touched it lightly with the toe of his boot (which he then lied about).
Why so close? the detective had asked. John didn't know, exactly. He
couldn't answer. Unlike you, John thought now, as he watched the
detective examine the body, I do not see dead women every day.

"Flesh is frozen," Frank said. "She's been here awhile."

"After the last snow, maybe," the sheriff said. "When was that?"

"Monday," one of the policemen said. "No, Tuesday night. A half
inch." It was Saturday.

"Maybe not," the detective said. "Snow could have blown or melted
off her. No tracks to her, either, 'cept for his."

"So how long she been here? About a week?" the sheriff asked.

Frank said, "Probably longer." He looked up at Paul and John. "I love
the winter. Body like this in the summer, flesh would be rotten and juicy.
I could push my finger through the skin, like breaking through the scum
on a bowl of gravy." He smiled at them. "Mosquitoes would be so thick
around the body I'd be breathing them in through my nose. Swat one
and you'd have her blood all over you." He flicked a finger against one
of the girl's arms. "See?" he said. "She's hard as a popsicle."

The sheriff's walkie-talkie buzzed and Buddy's voice echoed in the
cold.

"You there, sheriff?"

"What you have for us?"

"Becky Van Horn," he said, "age twelve, caucasian, four-foot ten,
seventy-one pounds, blond hair, blue eyes, inch-long scar on her chin.
Last seen walking home from Brandenberg Middle School, three forty-
five p.m. November eighteenth. What else you need?"

"That's it. Thanks."

"She the one?"

"Looks like our girl," the sheriff said.

Twelve years old. John felt his heart rise into his throat.

"Becky," the detective said. "Name's Frank Lyons." He was kneeling beside her, running a comb through her hair, scraping whatever he found into a plastic evidence bag. "Becky, honey, help us out here. Give us something. We'll get the bastard, but help us out."

"Sheriff?" one of the policemen called. "Something under the snow here. Underwear, maybe."

The sheriff took one of the evidence bags and went to where the policemen stood. He prodded with his pen and lifted a corn husk from the snow.

"False alarm," the sheriff said.

"That's my baby, Becky!" the detective shouted. He was holding tweezers. "Way to go, kid! Bill, we've got skin under these fingernails. Two or three nice slices."

The sheriff asked John, "Did you know the girl?"

"No," John said. "Not if she's that Van Horn girl. I read about her in the papers, though."

"You don't have to answer my questions," the sheriff said. "You can have a lawyer present."

"Why would I need a lawyer?" John asked.

"You're a suspect," he said. "Whenever a body is found, whoever finds her is a suspect. Standard police procedure. Don't get me wrong, I don't think you did it. But I have to ask you some questions." He pointed to the detective. "He's going to ask you some questions. He might want a hair sample or something. You can have a lawyer present, is all I'm saying. It's up to you."

"I don't need a lawyer," John said. "I wouldn't know where to find one, anyway."

"What about me?" Elmer said. In his haste to leave the house, Elmer had left his teeth behind, and when he grinned at the sheriff John could see the fleshy pink of his gums.

"You too," the sheriff said.

"What about the rest of you?" Elmer asked. "We're all men here. Why are we suspects and not the rest of you?"

"That's right," Frank said, chuckling, to the sheriff. "We're all men here. Put the cuffs on us, sheriff."

"What about the fat wise-ass," Elmer said, pointing to Frank.

"Me?" Frank said, and laughed.

"Come on, Frank," the sheriff said. "Let's just get this over with."

~

For nearly an hour, while the detective examined the body and the police searched the surrounding area, the sheriff asked John and Elmer questions and wrote the answers into his notepad. John relaxed after a few minutes when he realized the questions were routine. When the sheriff was through, he also relaxed, talked in a more friendly manner to them. He told them he'd been in police work for thirty-five years, and had reached the point in his career when he was happy, even thrilled, that when investigating a woman's murder, it was determined that the only indignity her body had suffered was to have the life drained from it by a bullet, a knife, or a rope. He said even in Clark County, with a population under fifty thousand people, he'd investigated the violent deaths of over a dozen women. Nearly every one of them was found in the woods. Two of them hanging from trees by their ankles.

The police found no other evidence in the surrounding area, and the detective was ready to roll the girl from her stomach to her back. The sheriff and one of the policemen put on rubber gloves to help him, because the girl was frozen to the ground. When they rolled her stiffened corpse to her side, frozen grass and dirt stuck to her body.

"Oh, shit," the policeman said.

John was so intent on looking for the small scar on the girl's chin—it was there—that he didn't immediately see the cause of the cop's reaction.

The detective was bent over, looking between the girl's frozen thighs. "It's a corn cob."

"God almighty," the sheriff said.

The girl's mouth was gagged with the sleeve of her blouse, but the detective peered under her chin and prodded with his fingers. "Rope burn. Looks like strangulation," he said. "I didn't find any bullet holes in her head, and I don't see any here. Another twenty minutes or so, and we can take her someplace warm, do the internal."

The paramedics smiled at this and stomped their feet on the ground.

"We'll get some blowers out here, the canine unit, get rid of some of this snow, see what else we can find."

"Sounds good," Frank said.

"Buddy," the sheriff said, into his walkie-talkie.

"Yeah, sheriff?"

"Get me the Van Horns' address, will you." He sighed and looked down at the girl. "We'll find the fucking bastard. I'd like to put his balls on a stick and roast them over a fire."

~

"Get anything, dear?" John's wife Alice asked, as he passed through the kitchen to the basement with his bow.

"Nothing," he said. "Didn't see any."

"Too bad. I'll warm you up some soup for lunch. It's twenty-one degrees, you must be an icicle."

As John undressed in the basement, draping his socks and gloves on the warm, steel, air ducts of the furnace, he thought about the sheriff driving up to the Van Horns in his squad car. He didn't know the family, but he'd seen their picture in the newspapers often in the past two weeks. Pictures of Becky Van Horn had been posted all over the city. Truckers had volunteered to post fliers at truck stops and restaurants throughout the state and the Midwest. Becky's mother, weeping on the ten o'clock news the night Becky was abducted, held an eight-by-ten photograph of her daughter in front of the camera, her seventh-grade school picture, and begged for her safe return. Becky smiled out from the photograph, a white lace collar around her neck, gold earrings shaped like dolphins shining in her ears.

The Van Horns had two children, Becky and a boy, Scott, age nine. The afternoon Becky disappeared, Scott had stayed after school to try out for the basketball team. Usually, he walked home with his sister. According to Becky's father, it was the first afternoon that quarter that the children did not walk home together.

As he removed his shirt, John saw the sheriff knock on the Van Horns' front door, his brown, round-brimmed hat clutched respectfully to his chest. He saw the inside door open, saw Mrs. Van Horn's fearful face through the glass, and her husband's stern face in the shadows behind her.

What did they think when they saw the squad car parked at the curb? Did they each rush to be the one to answer the door, or did each one hang back, hoping the other would face the sheriff first? Did they think it was hopeful news? Did they know in their hearts, after seventeen days without their daughter, in the cold of December, that it wasn't?

John put his slippers on and turned out the light. As he climbed the basement steps back to the kitchen, he imagined the sheriff saying how sorry he was, that a hunter had found their daughter's body, that he needed someone from the family to accompany him to the coroner's office to positively identify the girl.

In the kitchen, John sat down to a cup of coffee his wife poured him. He warmed his hands on the hot cup, and leaned over the sweet-smelling steam. He did not tell his wife what he'd seen that morning. He didn't know why.

On the six o'clock news, the discovery of Becky Van Horn's body was the lead story. A handsome reporter in a leather coat stood in the Franklins' snow-covered cornfield and explained that a hunter had found the girl's body in the woods behind him off County Trunk Y. Short interviews with the sheriff and the fat homicide detective followed. The sheriff said that as of now, there were no solid suspects in the case, and the detective said the crime scene was in excellent condition and unnamed evidence found with the body would help the investigation. The final story in the team report was an interview with a local psychic who had predicted the girl would be found in a snowy field by a hunter. The anchorman concluded the report by offering the station's condolences to the Van Horn family, noting that the family did not wish to comment at that time.

"That poor girl," John's wife said, when the stories were over. "What a world we live in."

~

That night John did not sleep well. Every time he closed his eyes he saw Becky Van Horn's frozen body, saw her glazed, open eyes, the gag across her mouth, her long, thin, feet, her tiny breasts. He wondered how long her body had been in the field. It was possible, he knew, that he'd walked past her many times as he made his way to his deer stand. It would be difficult, if not impossible, to ever walk Elmer Franklin's land again without thinking of the girl. She'd ruined his hunting there, forever. It was a selfish thing to even think about, he knew, but it was true. He'd spend no more quiet, peaceful hours sitting in those woods, not with the ghost of Becky Van Horn sleeping in the field.

When John finally fell asleep, he slept fitfully. He dreamed he was in some strange woods, the trees taller than any trees he knew, so tall they blocked out the sky, the sun. In every direction, the woods looked the same. There were no landmarks to comfort him, no fences, no nicely squared-off forties of corn or soybeans. The deeper he walked into the woods, the colder it became. His fingers and toes ached. His eyes teared beneath his glasses.

Then far ahead of him, he thought he saw something glowing— sunlight, perhaps, breaking through the trees, or the cozy warmth of a campfire. He hurried toward the light, which, as he got closer to it, seemed to radiate from behind every tree. He walked for minutes, for hours. But when he reached the place, he was repelled, in horror, by what he found. On the ground behind every tree, glowing like a harvest moon, was the nude body of a woman, hands bound, mouth gagged. Frantically, John went from body to body with his knife, cutting the rope from their hands, fumbling, with stiff fingers, to untie the cloth that stretched across their mouths. For each body cut free, another appeared, hundreds, thousands of bodies. And each was as cold as porcelain.

John awoke with a start, bathed in sweat, his heart thumping against his ribs. He sat up in bed and reached for his glasses. It was almost two o'clock in the morning. Next to him, his wife slept on her side, wrapped in the down comforter, breathing slowly and deeply.

When his heartbeat slowed, John carefully left the bed and pulled his cold clothes on over his pajamas. He sat in a chair in the dark and pulled on his socks, then his shoes. The stairs creaked as he walked stiffly down to the kitchen. He turned on the light, squinted his eyes in the sudden brightness. He opened one of the drawers and pulled out the telephone book, then sat at the kitchen table and opened the book to the

Brandenberg listings. Under V, he found Van Horn, and circled the address with a pencil. Then he flipped back to the first of the yellow pages, found the crude map of the city of Brandenberg, and put a star by the Van Horns' address.

He took his keys from the top of the refrigerator, pulled on his coat, hat, and gloves, and left the house.

Driving county roads in the dark, when no other cars were on the road, was one of John's favorite activities. In years of hunting, he'd found mysterious pleasure in waking before all but the farmers, in driving alone in the dark to the woods, the only human light radiating from milking barns he passed along the way. Sometimes, he thought, he enjoyed that dark, lonely drive, with his truck warm, the radio playing softly, tuned to a country station, even more than the hunt itself. There was a settling peace in it, in knowing that soon light would come, and others would swarm from their houses to join him in the world, driving to work, dropping kids at school, shopping.

Now, at two o'clock in the morning, stars glowed in the clear, cold sky, pinpoints of light in the velvety darkness. The heater fan hummed under the dash, and the warm air crowded the chill from the cab of John's truck. It was a bitterly cold night. Icy wind rushed against the windshield.

Brandenberg was twenty-three miles away, but it seemed to John that in no time he was coasting into the city, past the white, wooden sign that welcomed visitors. John put on the dome light to check the map, then clicked it off and turned right off the main street, past a small playground, furnished with a single, swingless swingset and a steel merry-go-round illuminated by streetlights. Three blocks later, he turned left. Just ahead of him, without seeing an address, he recognized the Van Horns' home, and turned off his lights. Although it was past two-thirty in the morning, it seemed as if every light was on inside and outside the house. No one there, it appeared, was sleeping through this terrible night. Six or seven cars were parked in the driveway. Two more rested at the curb.

In the front corner of the yard, three shadowy pine trees, thick across the bottom and almost blue in the translucent light, grew together inside a weathered, split-rail fence. John parked at the curb beside them, his truck hidden from the house. He turned off the engine, and waited.

No one pulled back curtains or opened the door to see him, so he breathed easier, undetected. He huddled deeper into his coat to ward off the creeping cold, put his hands in his pockets, and stared at the house.

He felt foolish, even a bit worried, that his wife might wake up and find him gone. But he relaxed when he realized she would roll over, content with the thought that he'd simply left for the deer woods a bit earlier than usual.

But his own doubts were not so easily dismissed. What was he doing here? What did he want? Maybe only this: to know someone could survive the news this family had received that afternoon. Did they know all he knew? More? Surely, they could not avoid the questions. What had been done to her, and when? What had Becky Van Horn been thinking? Had she known, when pulled from that familiar sidewalk, what awaited her? Had she called for her mother? Her father?

As the engine ticked and cooled beneath the hood, John slowly opened the door of his truck, stepped down to the street, and slowly closed the door, leaning on it with his hip until the latch clicked softly. He ducked around the back of the truck and then crouched, duck-walked, into the stand of pines. He dropped to his knees there, in the fragrant needles, sheltered from the snow, and hid behind the branches.

He thought about how the Van Horns' house might look from an airplane passing high overhead. People in the airplane might see the lights in the otherwise dark neighborhood and think someone was having a party. John had flown only once in his life, to Missoula, Montana on an elk-hunting trip his wife and children had given to him for his fiftieth birthday. He landed at ten o'clock at night, and had marveled at all the lights, how the whole city glowed from a distance. He thought then that even he could have steered the airplane in the right direction, coasting down out of the night sky to a safe, bright runway.

The Van Horns owned a simple, older home, a story and a half, the chalky aluminum siding pocked by hail. A small, three-season porch jutted out the front. John could visualize the inside from the details outside. Downstairs was a kitchen, living room, dining room, and family room. The bathroom and bedrooms were upstairs. The garage was out back, at the end of a narrow concrete driveway, and had a basketball hoop and backboard mounted on the roof. A television antenna rose from the peak of the house, its tripod discolored by rust, the flat wire flapping in the wind.

John's legs grew stiff, so he stood up again, holding pine boughs away from his head. This is stupid, he thought. I could get arrested. What the hell am I doing here? He fumbled with the keys in his pocket and thought about going home. He saw people passing behind curtained windows, watched smoke and steam from the furnace billow out the chimney. The cold was starting to chill him. His thighs, his hands and feet, his face, were going numb.

But when he stepped free of the trees, he did not follow the shadows back to his truck. He stepped forward, into the light. He took two cautious steps toward the house, breathed deeply, and continued. He left tracks in the snow until he reached the sidewalk, then turned and approached the house. He walked slowly up three concrete steps and stood at the front door. At his feet was a reed welcome mat with WELCOME FRIENDS woven into it.

He stood there, silently, his warm breath steaming circles on the glass of the door. He kept his hands in his pockets. Inside, he could hear floors creaking, calm voices. Then someone noticed him. A hand on a curtain, a concerned face, a flurry of footsteps growing louder.

"Who is it?" someone said.

The inside porch door opened and a man stood on the warm side of the glass, looking at him.

"Yes?" the man said. "Yes?"

John didn't know what to say. "I came here," he began. "I was passing through here. . . . No, I wasn't."

"He's drunk," someone said.

"A religious nut," said another.

John heard other voices. "Goddamned reporters. Who could it be at this hour? Maybe his battery went dead."

Behind the man at the door, a young woman appeared. The man stepped aside, allowed her to duck under his arm and walk past him into the porch. When John saw her, he was stunned. He held his breath to keep it from fogging his view of her face. The woman was Becky's mother. She looked exactly like her beautiful daughter.

"Yes?" she said. She looked directly at him, her eyes locked, unblinking, on his face.

"Get lost, buddy," someone far behind her was saying. "Bars are closed so go back home."

"I'm . . . I'm . . . here," John said, searching for the right words. But they wouldn't come to him. He turned, looked longingly at his truck, as if by seeing it he might transport himself into it and be gone. When he looked back at the woman, she was fumbling with the lock on the door.

"No," Becky's mother said, to the others. "No, it's all right."

John became aware of his hands shaking inside his pockets, of his knees quivering, his teeth clicking together. He felt the rush of warm air rise up his face as the woman opened the door. She looked up into his wet face, took his elbow, pulled him inside.

"It's cold," she said. "You must be freezing."

John nodded only, as he stepped over the threshold, and went in.

About the author

Ron Rindo was born and raised in Muskego, Wisconsin. He received his B. A. in English from Carroll College and his doctorate in American Literature from the University of Wisconsin-Milwaukee. After teaching at Birmingham-Southern College in Birmingham, Alabama for three years, Mr. Rindo returned to Wisconsin. He presently teaches English at the University of Wisconsin-Oshkosh and lives in Berlin, Wisconsin with his wife and twin children.

Mr. Rindo's first collection of short stories, *Suburban Metaphysics*, won the 8th Minnesota Voices Project Competition and was published by New Rivers Press in 1990. The collection, which received critical acclaim, was selected for Outstanding Achievement Recognition by the Wisconsin Library Association in 1991.

About the cover artist

The cover of *Secrets Men Keep* features "West Eightieth," a monoprint by Dyan McClimon-Miller. She was born in Davenport, Iowa and received a M.A. and a M.F.A. in Studio Art from the University of Iowa. A resident of Minneapolis for thirteen years, she taught at North Hennepin Community College, Macalester College, and the University of Minnesota, and she was represented by the Peter M. David Gallery. Ms. McClimon-Miller has exhibited regionally and nationally, and she currently lives in Oshkosh with her husband Scott where she teaches Design and Studio Art at the University of Wisconsin-Oshkosh.